KEN CANFIELD

THEY CALL ME

DAD

The Practical Art of

Effective Fathering

HOWARD BOOKS
A DIVISION OF SIMON & SCHUSTER
New York   London   Toronto   Sydney

This book reiterates the fact that Ken is the go-to guy for dads who want to be their very best. There is no sharper cutting-edge fathering book in the industry today.

— BILL BEAUSAY, Author, *Boys! Girls!* and *Teenage Boys!*

Every once in a great while there appears a practical no-nonsense book that cuts right through to the critical issues of fathering. They Call Me Dad *is that book. If you want your kids to lovingly "call you Dad," this book will set you on the spiritual, emotional, and relational path to make that a reality in your life.*

— DR. JUDSON SWIHART, LSCSW; Director, Cornerstone Family Counseling Center; Author, *How Do You Say 'I Love You?'*

They Call Me Dad *is a gift to every man who is tired of theory and wants to know what being a great dad looks like. I promise you that when you put this book down, you will be motivated, encouraged, and equipped as never before to become the kind of Dad you want to be and that your kids both need and deserve.*

— GARY J. OLIVER, PhD; Executive Director, The Center for Relationship Enrichment; Professor of Psychology and Practical Theology, John Brown University; Coauthor, *Raising Sons and Loving It!*

Exactly the book that today's dads need: practical and easy-to-read, yet grounded on eternal principles and faith that take a man beyond the 'see-it, fix-it' approach to fathering. First-time readers will find themselves catching their breath on the fresh ideas; re-reading will be like taking a breath of oxygen in a long race or game. If our nation is going to outlove, outthink, and outlive the self-serving culture of the day, They Call Me Dad *must be the map on the road less traveled. A must-read for all dads.*

— BEN SILLIMAN, PhD; Associate Professor and Youth Development Specialist, North Carolina State University

TO DADS OF DESTINY,
who are being transformed
by the grace of another Father
into true heroes of their children
and their children's children and . . .

HOWARD
BOOKS

Published by Howard Books, a division of Simon & Schuster, Inc.
1230 Avenue of the Americas, New York, NY 10020
www.howardpublishing.com

They Call Me Dad © 2005 by Ken Canfield

Library of Congress Cataloging-in-Publication Data
Canfield, Ken R.
  They call me Dad : the practical art of effective fathering / Ken Canfield.
     p. cm.
  ISBN 10: 1-58229-468-2; ISBN 13: 978-1-58229-468-1
  1. Fathers. 2. Father and child. 3. Fatherhood. 4. Fatherhood--Religious aspects--Christianity. 5. Parenting. I. Title.

HQ756.C3593 2005
248.8'421--dc22

                                                                    2005046066

11 10 9 8 7 6 5 4 3 2

HOWARD is a registered trademark of Simon & Schuster, Inc.

Manufactured in the United States of America

For information regarding special discounts for bulk purchases, please contact: Simon & Schuster Special Sales at 1-800-456-6798 or business@simonandschuster.com.

Edited by Liz Heaney
Interior design by John Mark Luke Designs
Cover design by The DesignWorks Group

CONTENTS

ACKNOWLEDGMENTS

During one of the busiest times of my life, I was challenged to write this book as a testimony to the transforming impact another Father was having in the lives of fathers across the globe.

While completing the manuscript I have been inspired by my enthusiastic publisher at Howard. The entire family at Howard Publishing, Denny and Philis Boultinghouse, John and Chrys Howard, Susan Wilson, Greg Petree, and their outstanding team have been a delight to partner with. They are committed to serving their authors, readers, and suppliers with excellence. I am grateful they secured Liz Heaney to be my editor. Liz was exceptional in shaping the structure and flow of ideas presented in this book.

Behind the scenes many people have had considerable influence on my thinking, writing, and speaking over the years. Randall Nulton labored a dozen years alongside me before passing away six months ago. He prayed and believed that the spiritual work of fathering would have a prominent role in shaping the fathers of this generation. Well, Randall, I believe that too, and this book is my two cents worth.

Brock Griffin has been the consummate servant to me and to thousands of other dads. Brock has collected, refined, and recorded the best fathering ideas for more than fourteen years. I rarely write anything for public viewing without Brock's input and support. So, Brock, we have another one in the can. Are you ready for more?

The National Center for Fathering creates a work environment vital to the entire fathering movement. The staff at NCF works out of a sense of calling. Peter Spokes and Ron Nichols left the corporate culture to pursue their passion, and they have produced much fruit. George Williams and Amos Johnson III are faithfully plugging away to erase the negative influence of fatherlessness from our urban communities. Bea Peters, Cathy Henton, Jeanette Ross, Steve Wilson, Alissa Lew, Lucy Bloom, and Kym Kiriakos all labor diligently, contributing their gifts and heartfelt services to benefit fathers. May each of you be rewarded in intangible ways for contributing to this important and significant work.

Recently Brian Bloomberg and Randy Phillips joined NCF to expand our efforts to engage fathers in a significant way, so stay tuned.

Since the founding of NCF, many others have served for a season and made important contributions. I am thankful for the service of Lowell Bliss, Marshall Hollingsworth, Bernard Franklin, David Warnick, Ken Howard, Ray Mabion, Rahn Franklin, Mike Randall, Karen Smith, Amy Wilson, Lyle Moss, Bill Beahm, Roy Quilice, and Bain Culton.

In addition, the board of directors of the National Center for Fathering serves out of a sense of duty and calling. Each board member has been successful in his field or business, yet they all know that being a dad and granddad is one of their most cherished roles. I am grateful for the service of Blake Ashdown, Joel Jennings, Rich Hosley, Lee Paris, Sam Mathis, Brian Wink, and Peter Spokes, as well as former board members Rick Thaemert, Dana Green, and Ron Rice. Thank you for giving sacrificially with your time and treasures.

My most important earthly treasures are locked up in relationships. As my mother has said, "I don't know where Ken would be if he hadn't met Dee." You're right, Mom. Dee has been a faithful friend, wife, and partner for thirty years. She has given birth and care to all of our five children. They are all signs to me that this world is in good hands. I look forward to another thirty years of serving with you Dee, Lord willing.

Rachel, Sarah, and Hannah, your character, service, and beauty are a joy to behold. May your heavenly Father provide everything you need in the coming years.

Micah and Joel, you are both stand-up gentlemen. I watch with excitement as the work of another Father unfolds in your lives.

Ted Mabie and Justin Heimer, it's great to have you on the team. May your fathering be filled with the same joy I have experienced as a father.

Finally, to the dads we serve at NCF who continue to inspire and challenge us. May the heavenly Father use this meager text to encourage you as a dad just as He has encouraged me. May His glory continue to be expressed in our weakness, and may His will be done in our hearts as He has modeled for us.

A CALL TO ACTION

See, I have set before you today life and good,
death and evil. . . . Therefore choose life, that
you and your offspring may live.
DEUTERONOMY 30:15–19

Dad, we are standing at a crossroads. Each of us faces a choice about our fathering that will either make or break the next generation.

Consider the following:

- Children growing up in a home without a dad are much more likely to: get in trouble with the authorities, drop out of school, make poor grades, commit delinquent acts, engage in drug and alcohol use, receive welfare, marry early, and go through a divorce as an adult.[1]

- Almost 60 percent of all children under the age of eighteen will spend at least part of their childhood living apart from their fathers.[2]

- In one study 53 percent of Americans agreed with the statement "Fathers don't know what is going on in their children's

1

lives," and 54 percent agreed that "most people [adults and children] have unresolved problems with their fathers."[3]

- Marie Bracki, associate professor of psychology at National-Louis University in Chicago, observes, "The gang is fulfilling the father role in the lives of youth! There is no use in trying to intervene in gangs if that intervention doesn't include a father figure."[4]

However:

- Infants who have time alone with Dad show richer social and exploratory behavior than do children not exposed to such experiences. They smile more frequently in general, and they more frequently present toys to their dad.[5]
- Children who feel a closeness to their father are twice more likely to enter college or find stable employment after high school, 75 percent less likely to have a teen birth, 80 percent less likely to spend time in jail, and half as likely to experience depression.[6]
- A four-decade study found that when dads encouraged their daughters to excel and achieve and were emotionally close to their sons, the daughters were more successful in school and in their careers, and the sons achieved greater status later in life.[7]

The data is sobering. The absence of a father leaves a child at risk, with hopelessness and disaster waiting in the wings. But the presence of a dad, particularly one who is warm and loving, can breathe hope and life into a child. What's more difficult to track is the impact of a dad who lives at home with his family but has not made fathering a priority in his life. While the situation may look better on the outside, over time these dads can cause the same pain as defacto dads.

No question about it: Every child needs a dad they can count on!

I believe that Moses's words to the nation of Israel as they prepared to enter the Promised Land can be applied to our nation today. "Dads, your attention to fathering will either yield life and good to your child, or death and evil. Therefore choose life so that you, your children, and your children's children may live!"

MAKE A COMMITMENT TO FATHERING

Dad, if you do not become attentive and involved in the lives of your children, you are putting them at risk. It is your God-given responsibility—and your privilege—to be the best father you can be to your children.

Perhaps you're wondering if this is even possible because you grew up without a dad or with one who was uninvolved or even abusive. Maybe someone told you that you live under a generational curse, one that you will inevitably pass on to your own children. If so, don't believe it. More important is your commitment to fathering today, tomorrow, and the rest of your life.

For at least the past three generations, the fathers in my family have not made spiritual growth a priority of the family. My great-grandfather, grandfather, and father were awesome, law-abiding, bring-home-the-bacon men, but when it came to the spiritual and emotional areas of their lives, they were quiet. When the heavenly Father transformed my heart, I soon discovered many other "spiritual fathers" who brought me guidance in a way my forefathers did not. I quickly learned that God was using these pastors and leaders as His fathering gifts to me in human form. All of them had families of their own, but it did not hinder them from sharing their lives with others. They provided the *spiritual care* that I needed.

God will bring men into your life who will do the same for you. All you need to do is ask Him. I am convinced that our heavenly Father will give His wisdom to any dad who hungers for His grace and mercy. Such a father will have a positive and lifelong impact for good in the lives of his children—no matter his own heritage.

This was true for me and also for pastor and writer Frederick Buechner. When Buechner was only ten years old, his father committed suicide. Over the course of his life, he learned that his heavenly Father brought healing to his life in ways he had only dreamed of, particularly in regard to his fatherless past. In his memoirs, *Telling Secrets*, Buechner wrote this about his father's death: "Who knows how I might have turned out if my father had lived, but through the loss of him all those long years ago, I think that I learned something about how even tragedy can be a means of grace that I might never have come to me any other way."[7] No clear-thinking person invites tragedy to his door, yet Buechner's story demonstrates the *curse reversed*—grace and blessing for forthcoming generations through a heavenly Father whose heart is turned toward His child.

When we invest in the hearts of our children and seek God's best for their lives, we are sending a powerful blessing into our world as well as to future generations. Our influence can be *exponential*. Here's an example of what I mean.

I have 5 children. If each of my kids has 3 children, and each of those grandchildren has 3 children, my fathering choices will likely influence at least 65 people. Add two more generations, and the number grows to 605 people—and that doesn't count the people outside my immediate family that my descendants will impact.

What kind of influence can we fathers have if we band together and make healthy fathering a passion in the land? Let's assume that at least ten thousand dads read this book. Even if we reduce the number of kids per family to an average of 2.5, we dads still have the potential to influence 62,500 grandchildren and 156,250 great-grandchildren. That's a decent-sized city! Carried out to the fifth generation, we can positively impact more than 1,000,000 descendants. We serve a God who is greater than you can imagine, and He has equipped you to be the father your kids need—starting today.

As fathers we need to promote an ethic, a movement, and a lifestyle that engages our faith and our fathering. This movement calls us to make being a father one of the highest acts of spiritual service, because unless we have renewal, our nation's legacy will be brokenness and suffering instead of blessing. However, if we take action, we can bring life and renewal to our households and restore the land. Our children and their children will thrive, and future generations will celebrate our faithfulness. Our legacy will be rich and filled with hope.

This book is an invitation to leave such a legacy. It's the result of fifteen years of research about integrating faith and fatherhood, and it seeks to show you how you can become a modern-day hero in the lives of your children by implementing nine key practices.

In 1990, after informally studying fatherhood for a number of years, I founded the National Center for Fathering as an outreach to equip today's fathers with the tools they need to become dads of destiny. Our goal is to make fathering a personal and national priority with the vision that no child would go unfathered. I'm convinced that many of today's dads are searching for answers about how to effectively father their families. It's time for a spiritual infusion of the Father's grace to engage dads and prompt their labor with fresh vision, passion, and discipline in their households and churches. Ultimately, these dads will have a life-giving impact on future generations.

As fellow pilgrims on the adventure of fatherhood, let's do everything humanly possible to succeed in our role as dads. At the end of our lives, the peace and satisfaction that come from being a committed father will have no rival. At that time we will feel the touch of another Father, and we'll hear Him say, "Well done, my good and faithful servant. I called many people to different tasks, but I called you to be a dad of destiny. You fulfilled your calling with excellence. Good work! Come join Me in glory."

HOW TO USE THIS BOOK

After reviewing this book, my colleague Dr. Walter Schumm wrote, "*They Call Me Dad* is a firehose experience of information that is best consumed one chapter at a time." I agree. In addition, it has been my experience that processing fathering information is done best in a small group. According to the research done by the National Center for Fathering, dads who are involved in a regular small group have fewer sexual struggles, report fewer problems with dishonesty, and are more connected on a spiritual level with their families. This confirms the many testimonies I have heard over and over from fathers. Meeting with other men for mutual support and encouragement is one of the best investments you can make to strengthen yourself as a dad.

Fathering requires action. It's more than knowing the right information; it's applying that information. It helps when you have someone putting pressure on you each week by saying, "So, what did you do about what we discussed last week?"

At the end of each chapter I have included three tools that can be used by individuals but are most effective when used in the context of a small group: a profile titled "Meeting the Challenge," which has been developed from surveys taken by thousands of fathers over the past ten years, asking them specific questions about their fathering behavior; a set of questions for discussion within your small group or for personal reflection; and a collection of action points that I have collected from other fathers who are also seeking to become dads of destiny.

I encourage you to join a small group soon—or start one of your own. Men who are seeking to become dads of destiny need each other. Dads need other dads who are willing to listen, exchange ideas, provide support, and give accountability to one another. If this happens, a movement will be born.

DADS OF DESTINY

My grace is sufficient for you, for my power is
made perfect in weakness.

2 CORINTHIANS 12:9

For several summers, I had the opportunity to lead groups of dads and their teenagers on a wilderness expedition sponsored by an outdoor adventure organization. It was a five-day getaway from civilization—no cell phones allowed—so dads and kids could renew their relationships while facing challenges together. Not only did they have a great experience together, most came away with a new perspective on their relationship and what's most important in life.

Each day's schedule included a fun and challenging activity, such as hiking, rappelling, or swimming, and a one-to-one dad-child dialogue designed to help dads practice the fine arts of listening and encouraging their kids. On day four, the dialogue focused on the child's goals and dreams. The dads helped their adolescent children set goals for the coming year and then made a commitment to help them reach their goals. Then each dad read a letter of blessing that he wrote to his child the previous day. In addition the dads gave their children similar letters from their moms, a friend, sibling, teacher, youth pastor, or other significant persons. That same evening the dads gathered for a special campfire to prepare for the next day's hike to a mountain summit where they would pronounce a specific blessing over their daughters.

One summer on a trip involving dads and daughters, I was struck once again by the profound effect of a father opening up his heart to his child. On the fourth night, as the dads were heading toward the sleeping bags, they were eager but also apprehensive. Clearly, this adventure was stretching them in ways they hadn't been stretched before.

Not one of these men had ever received a blessing from his own father. Most of them came from homes where the father had been present but not connected in a spiritual or emotional way. Nevertheless, each agreed that although verbally blessing his daughter in front of the entire group would be a challenge, it was the right thing to do. Clearly, many of those dads needed to *speak* the blessing as much as their daughters needed to *hear* it. Some of them would take a huge step by breaking the curse of silence in their families; others would take a good relationship with their daughter to a much deeper level.

It rained during the night, and morning brought a chilly wind—not uncommon in the Sierras, even in August. It would take about four hours of steep climbing to reach the summit. En route many of the girls complained: "I'm tired." "Let's go back." "How much farther?" As the hours passed, the tension increased. A few of the dads even suggested that we turn back.

But when we finally reached the top, something extraordinary occurred. The blustery wind suddenly died down, the clouds parted, and rays of sunshine burst through, almost like a spotlight. It was as if we were on holy ground. For the next hour, the air stayed calm and warm.

Then one by one each father introduced his daughter, shared something special about her, and pronounced a blessing on her in front of the rest of us. Next, all the fathers gathered around the dad and daughter and prayed that God would bring the blessing to pass. As each father shared—talking about his pride in his daughter, her unique gifts, and his love for her—he broke down and wept at some point, no exceptions. The daughters, who had been weary and grumbling, all became attentive and bright-eyed. After hearing her father speak blessings to her, each one was relaxed, talking, and laughing. I still hear from dads and daughters who talk about that day and the difference it made.

That experience—which happened on August 6, the same day the Eastern Church celebrates the Festival of Transfiguration—reminds me of one of the two times in Scripture when God spoke a blessing over His Son. Jesus, in preparation for His final days, had gathered three of His disciples to join Him for prayer on top of a mountain. There He was transfigured and joined by two heavenly visitors, Moses and Elijah. Then a cloud, signifying God's presence, covered the mountain, and God declared, "This is my Son, whom I love; with him I am well pleased. Listen to him!" (Matthew 17:5 NIV). Through this blessing, God affirmed His love for His Son and that He had chosen His Son to carry out His purpose.

> Fatherhood must be at the core of the universe.[1]
> C. S. LEWIS

That day on the mountain, those fathers did something similar for their daughters. Though their own fathers hadn't modeled this for them, these dads were willing to be vulnerable and bless their daughters. The transfigured impact was glowing young women with sparkling eyes.

Above all, each of these fathers made a commitment to forge a better relationship with his daughter and to become what I call a "dad of destiny." Dads of destiny are committed to being engaged fathers who bring life and renewal to their households so that their children—and future generations of children—thrive.

Dads of destiny father intentionally. They recognize being a dad is a gift from God that requires focus and faith. Dads of destiny are deliberate in setting goals and have plans to help their children succeed, but they also know it's not just about their desires. Rather, it's about being a servant to their children, ultimately submitting their hearts, minds, and wills to another Father. And by faith, over time, this heavenly Father will guide His earthly representatives to become dads of destiny in their homes, their communities, their country, and the world.

If we want to become dads of destiny, it will require three qualities or attitudes I observed in those dads on the mountain: vulnerability, passion, and an Abba connection.

COURAGEOUS VULNERABILITY

None of us are perfect. I fail in many ways as a dad, and I've tried to be honest and open about that with my family. But since few of us saw that openness in our dads—and being vulnerable and broken runs counter to our own egos and the image of success we try to uphold—the effort to be open and honest can be a challenge. But as fathers committed to connecting and building relationships with our children, we need to take this step if we want to unleash God's power in our families.

Through the apostle Paul, God tells us not to be concerned about weakness because, "My grace is sufficient for you, for my power is made perfect in weakness." Paul was so convinced of this that he proclaimed, "I will boast all the more gladly about my weaknesses, so that the power of Christ may rest on me. . . . For when I am weak, then I am strong" (2 Corinthians 12:9–10).

Strong, effective fathers admit when they are wrong. They are not afraid to say to their families, "I was wrong." "I'm sorry." "Will you forgive me?"

Ironically, confessing our *inadequacies* makes us more able to pass on an authentic legacy of faith to our children. Fortunate are the children whose dads recognize their own weaknesses and limitations and then lay them at the foot of the cross. You'll gain much credibility with your kids if you can tell them something about your own struggles and even ask them to pray for you. By demonstrating vulnerability and teachability, you will show them it's OK to make mistakes and that spiritual maturity is a lifelong pursuit. One of the most courageous things a dad can do is set aside his ego, admit his mistakes, and ask for forgiveness.

RELENTLESS PASSION FOR GOD

If you are going to become a dad of destiny, if you are going to be a hero to your kids, you will need to cultivate an inner drive, a God-given passion, to live a holy life before your children, and to prepare them for the challenges of life.

Many dads wilt in the face of the huge challenges. We freeze up or run away, when instead, we should act courageously through trust in the living God. Or, perhaps worse, we let our jobs or other pursuits distract us from what is most important. We may get lulled into complacency and overlook the challenges and changes that are coming in our children's lives—even though we say we want to make our kids a priority. But a dad of destiny wants to be certain that his child has a solid reference point for how a godly man lives, for oh so soon his daughter will be wooed by young men and his sons will be relating to young women and facing a variety of temptations.

First Samuel 17, which tells the story of David and Goliath, puts our challenge into perspective. David was the only one in all of Israel who was willing to fight the giant. Why? Because he was a man of great passion for the Lord. When he got to the camp, he immediately saw that something wasn't right. "Who is this . . . ," he asked, "that he should defy the armies of the living God?" (v. 26). Then, when facing Goliath, he risked everything on God. He said, "Today the whole world will know that there is a God in Israel . . . for the battle is the LORD's, and he will give all of you into our hands" (vv. 46–49 NIV).

Do you have a giant that needs to be slain? A difficult relationship with a teen, a personal struggle or addiction, or an uncontrollable temper? Sometimes it's scary just relating to our kids and opening our hearts to them. Have you been standing on the sidelines? Have you forgotten that you have God's power on your side?

In God's hands, a shepherd boy has a sling with perfect aim, and a scrawny kid can kill a giant and become a great king. And with God's power we dads can bring healing to relationships that seem hopeless. We can even change destructive habits that have been in place for generations.

Passion is proactive. It makes sure that first things do come first; it leads us to follow God, even at great risk. Dad, what giants are you facing today? Get your sling and rocks! Remember that God is bigger than any giant in your path. All you need is faith the size of a mustard seed and the courage to trust.

Maybe you didn't come to know the Father until your children were teenagers, and you have many regrets about how you have treated them in the past. Even so, God can bring about His full blessings to your children through your fathering.

Maybe you're seeking healing from a relationship with a father who was abusive, emotionally distant, or absent. Again, God will see that you are not shortchanged, but you must open your heart and by faith cry out, "Abba Father." He wants to bring healing to your life. Your heavenly Father knows what you need before you ask. Jesus said, "Which one of you, if his son asks him for bread, will give him a stone? Or if he asks for a fish, will give him a serpent? . . . How much more will your Father who is in heaven give good things to those who ask him!" (Matthew 7:9–11). When you open your heart to Him, He will give you what you need to be a great dad, whether it's healing from a rocky past, guidance for a current struggle with your child, or both. He wants to help you bless your children, give them a firm foundation, and create a climate in your home where their spirits will thrive.

If you had a good relationship with your father, you may be wondering why I'm placing such an emphasis on healing wounds from the past. We are all wounded sons, whether the wounds be mild or severe. No matter how great your dad may have been, he wasn't perfect. He had to let you down in some small ways. The gap between your father and an absent or irresponsible father is really much smaller than the gap between your father and your heavenly Father. Your heavenly Father has so much more in mind for you. So no matter what our fathering heritage may be, it falls short of what God intended. The healing agent of God's saving grace in our lives can enable us to be the fathers our children need.

But we can't be the father we want to be until we are first reconciled as sons. It is wise to reconcile our hearts and lives to the heavenly Father as a precursor for our work as fathers.

A HEART-TO-HEART CONNECTION WITH ABBA

Less than a week after God had blessed Him, Jesus was in the Garden of Gethsemane, wrestling with God over His forthcoming arrest and crucifixion. Mark records the prayer and cry of Jesus: "Abba, Father, all things are possible for you. Remove this cup from me. Yet not what I will, but what you will" (14:36). Many scholars and theologians agree that this represents a turning point in the way Jesus wants His followers to think about God. "For Jesus to venture to take this step was something new and unheard of. He spoke to God like a child to its father, simply, inwardly, confidently; Jesus' use of Abba in addressing God reveals the heart of his relationship with God."[2]

The apostle Paul explained what *Abba* meant in his epistles to the Romans and the Galatians. We really are children of God—"God has sent the Spirit of his Son into our hearts, crying, 'Abba! Father!'" (Galatians 4:6). When we cry, "Abba! Father!" the Spirit himself bears witness with our spirit that we are children of God (see Romans 8:15–16).

Jesus used His relationship to His Father as a model for us to follow. Jesus refers to God as "my Father" twenty-five times in the gospel of John. In doing so, He demonstrates His unique relationship with the Father, who is His source of guidance and strength. "The Son can do nothing by himself; he can do only what he sees his Father doing, because whatever the Father does the Son also does. For the Father loves the Son and shows him all he does. Yes, to your amazement he will show him even greater things than these" (John 5:19–20 NIV).

Later, Jesus introduced a new facet of the father/son relationship to the disciples. At the tomb, He tells Mary Magdalene, "Go . . . to my brothers and tell them, 'I am returning to my Father *and your Father*, to my God *and your God*'" (John 20:17 NIV, emphasis added). This proclamation offers hope of intimate relationship with our heavenly father.

Our Abba Father has demonstrated His love by being attentive and responsive to our needs as sons and our destiny as fathers. When we develop a heart-to-heart Abba-Father connection with God, our own approach to fathering will become attentive and responsive to the needs of our children.

Men, when you open your heart to the Father, His healing and empowering are as certain as the warm rays of a rising sun. And in due time, because of what He has revealed to you as His adopted son, you will set into motion authentic acts of fatherhood.

HEALED HEALERS

I've spoken with hundreds of men who were provoked and embittered by hostile or uncaring fathers. Maybe that was your experience. Now that you're a father, many of those negative memories and heated emotions may have come flooding back, leaving you unprepared to relate responsibly to your own kids. It's like you have a crippling wound, and that pain should not be trivialized.

However, you now have a heavenly Father, and by His power you can join the distinguished ranks of fathers whom I call "healed healers." These men successfully work through the issues of the past and move confidently into the future with their own children. They are willing to admit weaknesses, they're passionate about doing whatever it takes to connect with their children, and they are developing an Abba-Father relationship with God.

The following poem captures one dad's experience of finding spiritual healing for his father-wound:

One morning I stood at the window,
made cold from the outside rain,
and rubbed a circle on the steamy glass,
exposing beneath, the pane.

Through my circle, I saw my father
climb routinely into the car.
His job would keep him distant,
his work would take him far.

"Of course your father loves you.
Can't you see how he provides?
Just accept," my mother told me,
"that he keeps his love inside."

So I, too, learned the business
and made love a transactional art.
I sold my grades to buy his time.
I played sports to buy his heart.

Yet, I imagine that once my father
made his own circles on the pane.
I know his dad had left him.
He had not heard from him again.

And I imagine that, in his young heart,
he had made a solemn vow:
He would love his sons and give them time;
he would break the cycle now.

Yet despite his noble ambition,
my dad, too, soon became
another father, the circle unbroken,
the patterns still the same.

So as time passed by and our numbers grew,
I left home in my own car.
I never returned to mend the fences.
I never returned to start.

I never returned to share the pain I felt inside
and the grief I had learned to stuff.
No, it was more than I could handle,
but less than I could bluff.

Still, something inside me beckoned,
for I, too, had come of age.
I now had children of my own
that I had begun to encage.

No longer a boy, still I desired
a father's voice accepting of me.
Too often I wanted to scream and shout.
Too often I wanted to flee.

It was time to go, and wisely so,
to find that for which I yearned.
I couldn't make sense amidst the pretense
until I finally learned

That once, two thousand years ago,
the sky burst forth in rain.

It was a Son who had gone to work,
and a Father who felt the pain.

It was His whisper that drew me close,
a voice that caused no shame.
I found the Father of my great search,
and Abba is His name.[3]

The pain created by imperfect fathers is passed from generation to generation, but you can be the one to break the cycle. As you draw close to your Abba-Father, you will find the strength and faith to become a dad of destiny who makes a positive difference for generations to come.

I know men who lay their lives on the line for their kids, seeking to leave a legacy of love and grace. Their commitment to fatherhood, first as a son and then as a father, fashions them into healed healers. Simply defined, a healed healer is a dad who recognizes his weakness as the basis for his strength. By being transparent and vulnerable, he finds healing through the competence of another Father. Dads who recognize their weaknesses are more likely to reach out and ask for wisdom from above.

Healed healers are positioned to become healers for their children and for generations to come. And healed healers become the models of authentic fatherhood for their family and community in a simple yet profound way.

PREVIEWING THE PLAN

If we are going to restore fragile families and give our children the foundation they need, we can't settle for imitating the world or even merely surviving in the world. A dad of destiny understands that his call to be a father is a supreme act of spiritual service. He accepts the challenge in Romans 12:2, where Paul urges us not to conform to the world but to be transformed—in a way transfigured, by the love of our heavenly Father—so that we can demonstrate the good and acceptable will of God. To do so we need a new paradigm for fathering.

This paradigm is simple. It incorporates both sacred and scholarly insights and is designed to be a bugle call to arms for dads of destiny. Dad, I want to challenge you to cast a vision for your children's future by showing them how to *outlove the world, outthink the world,* and *outlive the world.*

We can *outlove* this world because the Father can give us His heart of compassion. One of the most loving gifts we have to share with others is the grace to forgive. God knows your sins and my sins, and He forgives them—as far as the east is from the west (see Psalm 103:12). He desires that we live like Him and extend His love and forgiveness to others. The world will know who we are and whose we are, by our love.

We can *outthink* the world because as devoted, obedient followers of Christ, we have something that even the most brilliant minds of the world can never grasp. We have the mind of Jesus, complete with His wisdom, insight, and wit.

We can *outlive* the world because we have the Holy Spirit, who can empower us. Sure, we're still human. We'll get sick and eventually die, but we're living with a new strength from above, and the quality of our life and our children's lives can set us apart from the rest of the world.

Now, you might say, "I'm no Einstein or Harvard grad. I'm just trying to get by. How do I outthink this world?" Or, "How am I going to outlive the world when I struggle with the same things everyone else does?" Maybe you have an addiction or a volatile temper or materialistic tendencies. Or, when it comes to love, "Dr. Canfield, don't ask me to step out of my comfort zone and reach out to an unfathered child." Or, "Don't tell me I have to forgive someone who hurt me really bad. You don't understand being abandoned and the pain that left in my life."

It's true—I *don't* understand your situation, but I know what God has done in my life and in the lives of so many friends and colleagues. So, as a fellow father, like one beggar telling another beggar where to find bread, I'm hoping to share what I've discovered. Throughout this book, I'll give you many ideas for how you can help your kids outlove, outthink, and outlive the world.

MEETING THE CHALLENGE

Commitment

A dad of destiny maintains a high level of motivation in his fathering and draws confidence from his role as dad. He claims his children verbally, resolves to always act on their behalf, and regularly invests his time, energy, and resources in their lives, giving them a high place on his list of priorities.

INSTRUCTIONS:

On a scale of 1 to 5, rank the accuracy of the following statements. Then add your scores and plot your total on the scale below. (You may want to have your child's mother or someone who knows you well take the survey and then compare their answers to yours. If your child no longer lives at home, score yourself as you remember your involvement.)

5 = Mostly True
4 = Somewhat True
3 = Undecided
2 = Somewhat False
1 = Mostly False

1. I avoid action in fathering my children. ☐

2. I tend to delay doing the things I know I should do as a father. ☐

3. I have difficulty in being motivated to do my fathering tasks. ☐

4. It is hard for me to get going in my fathering role. ☐

5. I rarely have time to play games with my children. ☐

6. My children and I seldom have time to work together. ☐

7. I rarely spend time with my children. ☐

TOTAL ☐

PLOT YOUR SCORE:

35	25	19	13	9	7
VERY POOR	POOR	AVERAGE	GOOD	VERY GOOD

(The scale is not uniform because it is based on norms from a study of 1,650 fathers.[4])
This is a reverse scale as the questions have been worded negatively.

QUESTIONS FOR DISCUSSION AND REFLECTION

As you consider how you scored on this inventory, think about the following questions or discuss them with some other fathers.

1. How did your father express his commitment to you? How did it make you feel?

2. What steps do you need to take to improve your communication with your children?

3. What are some specific things you can do to maintain your commitment to fathering?

4. Describe a man whom you consider to be a highly committed father. What makes him a good dad?

5. What sacrifices have you made—or do you need to make—for the sake of your kids?

ACTION POINTS

Choose one of the following action points and commit to doing it before you go on to the next chapter (or your next group meeting).

1. Skim through the gospel of John and identify ten times where Jesus refers to "my Father."

2. Ask your child what she'd like to do when she grows up and then set your own goals for how to help her.

3. Ask your wife or someone else who knows you well to suggest one area in which your fathering could use improvement.

4. When you go to work after hours, arrange for your children to come along.

5. Seek out an older father and ask him about the greatest struggle he has faced in his fathering and how he has handled it.

6. Skip lunch one day a week to pray for your children.

7. Ask your child what he likes to do with you and set a date to do that together.

8. Surround yourself with visual reminders of your commitment: photographs, your child's artwork, "World's Best Dad" mugs, T-shirts, and hats.

9. Be a chaperone at your child's next school function.

10. Find another man whom you can encourage in his fathering— and then do it.

PART ONE

Outloving
the World

As the men whom our children call Dad, our love must supercede what the world offers. The world's love comes with strings attached—with conditions and limitations. But a dad of destiny knows that the Father's love is limitless and capable of empowering him with an out-of-this-world ability to express grace, patience, and forgiveness to his family.

The loving father in Luke 15 is a true model for a dad of destiny. When one child walked away and the other developed an arrogant attitude—contrary to what they had been taught—this dad patiently and proactively outloved them by extending grace, forgiveness, and celebration. When times are tough, a loving father looks ahead to the day of celebration where he can rejoice in the rich relationship he shares with his children.

CHAPTER 2

FILL THEIR EMOTIONAL
CUPS

The Father of mercies and God of all comfort, . . .
comforts us in all our affliction, so that we may
be able to comfort those who are in any affliction, with the comfort with which we ourselves
are comforted by God.

2 CORINTHIANS 1:3–4

The football coaches at Gilman High School in Baltimore *get it*. It's
their custom at each practice and after every game to gather the team
around for a unifying team cheer. But they aren't saying, "Go
Greyhounds!" or, "Win," or even, "Together."

Instead, the coach yells, "What is our job as coaches?"

To which the boys reply, "To love us!"

"And what's your job as players?"

"To love each other!" they yell back.

This coaching style deeply impressed Pulitzer prize–winning author Jeffrey Marx, who wrote *Season of Life*. He followed the Gilman
team around for a year and heard the Gilman High mantra regularly.
He concluded, "If a Martian had just happened to land on Earth and
somehow found himself witnessing only that introductory talk, a perfectly logical communiqué home might have included a summary

such as this: 'Learned about some sort of group gathering called football. It teaches boys to love.'"[1]

Joe Ehrmann, a volunteer coach at Gilman who is also a pastor, teaches his players that loving and affirming each other is a powerful way to express their manhood. He says, "Most of us have a huge father pain somewhere deep down inside, a huge father longing because we have never been accepted, never been embraced the way we need to be."[2]

Ehrmann works from the assumption that loving his players in a strong, masculine manner will help them succeed in sports and, more importantly, in life. And it's clearly working. Gilman has finished three of the last six seasons undefeated and number one in Baltimore, and many of the young men in the program graduate with a clear sense of purpose: to go on to become responsible adults and positive contributors to society.

David, a linebacker on the team, wrote this when one of his teachers assigned the students to write their own obituaries: "David was a man who fought for justice and accepted the consequences of his actions. He was a man who would not allow poverty, abuse, racism, or any sort of oppression to take place in his presence. David carried with him the knowledge and pride of being a man built for others."[3]

David and his teammates are learning how to outlove the world.

In Colossians 3:12–14, Paul writes: "Clothe yourselves with compassion, kindness, humility, gentleness and patience. Bear with each other and forgive whatever grievances you may have against one another. Forgive as the Lord forgave you. And over all these virtues put on love, which binds them all together in perfect unity" (NIV).

When it comes to loving your children, no one on earth has more potential to make a difference than you, Dad. If we are going to teach our children how to outlove this world, we need to set the standard in regularly communicating our love for them.

I hope that one day I will be able to say, "There's a distinct quality I've noted among dads who follow Jesus. They express their fatherly love through blessing, encouragement, forgiveness, and comfort to such an extent that it becomes the foundation for their children's capacity to love others."

Will this happen? I hope so, but it will require supernatural surgery in the hearts of fathers. In seminars around the country, I often ask audiences this revealing question: "Did your father regularly express his love to you when you were growing up?" Rarely do more than 25 percent of the attendees raise their hands to signal *Yes*. Most dads are working from a deficit when it comes to love. If you didn't experience love through the blessing and caring arms of your father, it will be nothing short of the miraculous for you to express your love to your child.

If our ultimate goal is to see our children reach out to the world in love, we have to fill up their emotional cups so that they feel loved and secure and can go forth confidently to outlove the world. To do this we need to "grasp how wide and long and high and deep is the love of Christ, and to know this love that surpasses knowledge—that [we] may be filled to the measure of all the fullness of God" (Ephesians 3:18–19 NIV). Out of that fullness, we are able to follow the Father's example and give love abundantly to our children.

Children benefit greatly from a dad's unique, masculine approach to parenting. Men, we can and *must* overcome our past and whatever misguided cultural norms stand in our way to become nurturing dads.

Our children's self-esteem blossoms when we nurture them in appropriate ways. Your kids have a profound need for your physical affection, attention, affirmation, and loving actions.

SHOW THEM AFFECTION

I come from a long line of responsible, hard-working men. For my father, grandfather, and great-grandfather, physical and verbal affirmation were not important parts of their lives. They were men of few gestures and even fewer words. I cannot remember any hugging and very little touching between the men in my family, other than a rare handshake. They didn't say, "I love you," or, "I'm proud of you." Since I rarely saw a man display these nurturing qualities, such expressions of love don't come naturally to me. I have had to work hard to overcome my discomfort so that I can give my children the love they need.

I know I'm not alone. Affection is pretty simple to understand, but it isn't always easy to express. Sure, babies can fall asleep on your chest or in the crook of your arm in an instant. And when they get a little older, it's natural to roughhouse on the living-room carpet. But what about those awkward teenage years? Some dads are only comfortable giving a squeeze on the neck or a playful tousle of the hair. Maybe they think that meaningful touch lies more in the realm of motherhood than fatherhood.

But affectionate touch between a father and child creates a psychological bond. We can "say" things through physical touch that we can't say with words, and our children receive benefits from touch that they probably cannot comprehend, much less put into words. We ought to give displays of love for all to see and feel and smile about.

Boys and girls both need their father's affection, but studies have shown that fathers should use different approaches with sons compared to daughters.[4] To put it succinctly, girls respond to face-to-face affection and boys respond to shoulder-to-shoulder.

Daughters need face-to-face affection. Daughters tend to gain more when their dads demonstrate affection with hugs, kisses, and other loving expressions—often face-to-face. A girl's sense of worth as a woman is largely influenced by her relationship with her dad. When she's younger, it may seem natural to cuddle your cute little girl. Yet before you know it, she has become more than cute—more like a woman—and it may seem awkward to show her the same kind of affection you did when she was younger. But keep in mind that she's trying to figure out men, and you're her closest and best example of one. That's why she needs to continue to receive healthy affection from you. Instead of withdrawing from your daughter because of your discomfort—perhaps causing her to think, *Dad doesn't care,* or, *There must be something wrong with me*—you can show her what proper male affection sounds and feels like. By making your daughter feel accepted and loved, you'll also remove her need to look for that love and acceptance elsewhere—in all the wrong places.

Sons need shoulder-to-shoulder affection. Boys gain self-esteem from sustained contact, such as wrestling or other physical play, being picked up by their dad, sitting on his lap, or being held. And they need big, old-fashioned bear hugs and other displays of affection as well, on into adulthood. A father's display of warmth and security will build positive self-esteem in a son. Studies indicate that sons of sensitive, affectionate fathers score higher on intelligence tests and do better at school than sons of colder, authoritarian fathers.[5] They also have fewer gender identity issues.[6]

Something about physical touch makes us feel better, physiologically and psychologically. In one study at Purdue University, researchers asked the library staff to alternately touch and then not touch students' hands as they handed back their library cards. The study found that those students who were touched had more positive experiences in the library than those who were not.[7] And a classic study from UCLA found that people need eight to ten affirming touches a day for emotional health.[8]

How many affirming touches do you receive in a day? How many do you give to your children? Dad, the research is clear; your children are waiting. It may not come easy, but determine to start hugging, patting, rubbing, squeezing, and loving your children. Hold them in your arms. Include lots of loving physical contact as you interact and play together. Put your arm on his shoulder. Hold her face in both hands, and tell her how glad you are to be her dad. Show love to your kids as often and in as many ways as possible. Keep it up until it becomes the most natural thing in the world. Kids can't get enough of your love!

GIVE THEM YOUR UNDIVIDED ATTENTION

As fathers we need to be available and concerned for our children and to focus on their needs. When we take time to listen to their stories, thoughts, and opinions, we express love by showing that they deserve our full concentration—open ears, alert eyes, and clear minds—and that they are worthy to be known and understood.

All too often our kids lose out in competing for our attention. They get shoved aside for the newspaper, the computer, or the television. "Wait until I'm done with this one thing," we say, and the child stomps back upstairs. After all, we are preoccupied with important stuff, aren't we? And our children usually aren't talking about things all that important . . . are they?

In situations like this, what are your children really saying? If you have "ears to hear" and "eyes to see," you'll notice that they simply want to be with you. To them, it's the *telling* that's important, not so much the content of what they're saying. By patiently listening—with your eyes and ears—you can be alert to these times of "show and tell."

Children learn very quickly whether we are willing to listen to them. They may learn that when Dad's in his office, he's unavailable; better go ask Mom. Their concerns may be minor ones, and Mom may handle the situation quite effectively. But one day, they'll be teenagers who face bigger decisions—about a weekend party or the character of a new friend. If you've never really been around to listen to your kids in the past, it will be much more difficult to get them to open up when they really need your wise counsel.

Let's look at a few practical ideas on listening:

1. *Tune out all distractions.* Have you ever approached someone to tell him something only to hear him say, "OK, shoot. But make it short; I have to be somewhere." So you summarize what you wanted to say, but you end up trivializing something that's important to you. Meanwhile, your so-called listener is stealing glances at his watch. You decide to clam up altogether; there's no dignity in this kind of communication. How does it feel? That's how your children may feel sometimes.

   When your children are talking to you, put down the book or work project and turn off the stereo or computer game. Give them your full attention. Maintain eye contact and do your best to clear your mind. Make it obvious that you're available and free to listen, and you never know what you might hear your children say.

Granted, there are times when carving out enough time to listen to your children just isn't possible. A critical, prior commitment may prevent you from responding to their sudden request for your attention. But really, how often does that happen? Isn't it more likely that you put them off because you're a little tired or distracted, or you don't want to miss the dialogue on some television program? Dad, this is your flesh and blood! You'd give your life for them! Don't make them wait for the next commercial.

2. *Devote the time.* You've probably heard the old "quantity time" versus "quality time" debate. There are certain times when a child wants to talk, and if you're spending a lot of time together, you'll probably be available when those times arise. Also, it's more likely that conversations will occur when a father and child are just "hanging out to-gether." It isn't easy to say what's on your heart as you're standing in a crowded line at the amusement park, sharing some so-called quality time.

3. *Just listen, don't fix.* Maybe you're a real handyman around the house. No matter what the problem—a bike, a favorite toy, the kitchen faucet—you say, "Let me take a look." I believe part of that is our divine gifting as men. God blessed many of us with an understanding of how things work so we can restore order to our child's world, whether it's a broken toy or some larger crisis. Men tend to be very goal and objective oriented. Again, that sometimes works in our children's favor. But often it doesn't.

Let's say your daughter comes to you with a different kind of problem—a broken heart. If you try to fix it for her, like you would a faulty thermostat on your car, you'll come across to her as cruelly insensitive: "That's OK, honey. He wasn't right for you anyway. Now you can focus more on your schoolwork."

But often our best approach to a child's problems is to listen. Our kids may not need to know the smartest thing to *do*; they simply want to know that they're still accepted by the most important man in their life. And you demonstrate that by listening. Maybe, after listening, you can determine that what your child needs most is a big daddy bear hug, not advice.

4. *Use summary statements and clarifying questions.* Instead of trying to fix the problem or saying, "I understand exactly what you're feeling"—which could also bring a quick end to the conversation—draw out your children with summary statements and clarifying questions.

   For example, your son is talking about his frustration in chemistry class. He pauses for a second and looks at you. A summary statement can be something neutral, such as: "Hmm. I know how much you enjoy being in that class." This lets your son know you're with him, and he can continue.

   Or a clarifying question might sound like this: "OK, let's make sure I understand. You're upset because the other students are goofing off and you're not getting anything done?" Then your son can say, "No, not quite," and explain further, or say, "Yeah, that's right," and keep going with confidence that you're tuned in to his every word. It may seem awkward at first, but keep practicing. These valuable tools will help you better understand your children—and strengthen your bond with them.

5. *Listen for the agenda.* When people try to communicate, they have an agenda—something they hope to accomplish. For example, if your daughter comes to you and says, "I want pizza tonight," chances are she has told you exactly what her agenda is.

Problems arise for dads because many of us want the plain, cold facts, but our children don't always communicate that way. What if your daughter says, "Dad, I'm tired of school"? If you're too busy or too tired or too distracted to really listen to her, you won't recognize that there may be more on her agenda. If you say something to her like, "You don't have to like school, but you still have to go," you will send her a message that you don't want to listen anymore. The conversation will likely end, and your daughter will probably go away disappointed.

But if you can listen for her agenda, you'll look past the words and realize there's more she wants to communicate. "Tired of school?" you might ask. "You've always liked your teachers." This gives her a chance to respond and clarify. It may take several more interchanges before you finally get to her real agenda: her best friend is spending a lot of time with another girl, and she doesn't know how to handle it.

Remember, feelings are complex and multilayered. One item on your child's agenda may lead to another and then another. You might eventually find that your daughter is upset with you because you decided to move the family across town, and she had to change schools and leave her old friends. Those feelings can be discussed and resolved when they're out in the open, but only if you listen long enough to uncover the entire agenda. So, whenever your child speaks to you, try to keep this question in mind: *What's the agenda?*

SPEAK WORDS OF AFFIRMATION

Two of the most prominent occasions where God speaks in the New Testament occur when He is blessing His Son, Jesus. At His baptism, Jesus comes out of the water and a voice from heaven says, "You are my Son, whom I love; with you I am well pleased" (Mark 1:9–11 NIV). Then, at Jesus's transfiguration, the voice says again: "This is my Son, whom I love. Listen to him!" (Mark 9:7 NIV).

Gordon MacDonald has pointed out three valuable blessings that God the Father bestowed upon His Son at these two occasions.[9] We can communicate these same blessings to our own children.

First, God communicated *belonging*: "This is my Son," He said. What a difference it makes to our children when we claim them as our own! We communicate our acceptance of them and our pride in them, no matter what.

Next, God said, "whom I love." This communicates *value*. We want our children to know how deeply we care for them, whether they've just won a race or just disobeyed us. When we communicate value—both verbally and physically—our children can go forth with confidence.

Finally, God blessed Jesus by saying, "Listen to him!" These words bestowed *competence*. I've talked to many adults who are still trying to please their fathers. When we tell our children "Good job," "I'm proud of you," "Well done," we're showing that we recognize and appreciate their unique gifts. We are telling them that we believe in them—and we are helping them to learn to believe in themselves.

God gave His Son the blessings He needed. How much more do our children need those same blessings from us! A dad of destiny uses words to convey support, protection, comfort, encouragement, sympathy, tenderness, and caring. The way he interacts verbally with his children has a lasting effect, determining their level of security and their ability to empathize.

Words are a great tool for loving fathers. Unfortunately, if we are not thoughtful and proactive in our choice of words, they can also exasperate. Many children grow up never hearing the words "I love you" or "I'm proud of you" from their fathers. What they do hear is "If you work a little harder, you can turn that B into an A." These fathers mean well, but they convey a not-so-subtle message: "You can always do better." Even though that's true, how different it is for the child who hears this from his father: "How are you feeling about your grade? Do your best work, because your life is not based on performance alone. I love you because of who you are, not what you do."

Affirmation means verbally encouraging and blessing our children. I think of encouragement and blessings as distinct in this way: *Encouragement* typically has a reason behind it, like when you notice your child is upset or frustrated about something or has done something praiseworthy. *Blessings* can be purposeful and specific, but are often unconditional. Let's look at these two methods of affirmation.

1. *Encouragement.* Philippians 2:1 begins, "If you have any encouragement from being united with Christ . . ." (NIV). Those few words tell us that encouragement doesn't have to arise from a father's model or our own sense of well-being. It comes from our relationship with Christ. So even if we never heard any words of encouragement growing up, we can encourage our children.

Then, in 1 Thessalonians 2:11–12 we find this: "For you know that we dealt with each of you as a father deals with his own children, encouraging, comforting and urging you to live lives worthy of God" (NIV). Notice that Paul lists encouragement as one of the things a father does. So you might say it's your fathering destiny to be an encourager.

Here are some ways to start:

- *Do it verbally.* Notice and praise a job well done or progress in something your child is doing. Say "You can do it" or "I believe in you" as they are facing a challenge. Compliment both physical skills and character qualities, such as emotional strength, a sense of humor, loyalty, intelligence, and courage. And even as you gush over each of your children's gifts, make it clear that even without those features, you'd still love them just as much.

- *Write them letters, short notes, cards, and e-mails.* These can be read over and over. Sometimes all you have to say is "I was thinking about you today, and it made me happy to know I'm your dad."

Chris told me that he went on a summer trip with his daughter and the rest of her youth group. The purpose of the trip was to work on houses in a blighted rural area. As a bottom-line, results-oriented businessman, Chris was eager to get in there, swing a hammer, repair some walls, and get as much done as possible in the time they were there. But before they started, the project director explained that every day the first order of business was to write an "encouragram"—a short note of encouragement—to another team member. *What does this have to do with building houses?* Chris thought. Then about an hour later, he went to his envelope and found this message: "Thanks for coming along on the trip. I love you and am glad you're here." It was signed "Erika"—his daughter.

Over the next seven days, Chris wrote many notes to his daughter and the other youth on the trip, and he received many himself. It was an eye-opening reminder of the dynamic impact of encouragement, and since then he has committed himself to using encouragrams regularly at home with his wife and children.

• *Demonstrate confidence in their abilities.* You might share something you're working on and ask a child's opinion or assign a challenging task and express trust that the child can handle it. One woman who's now an engineer says, "Dad demonstrated that there was nothing I couldn't do." Remember, if your children know that you think of them as future achievers, you can change their whole outlook on the future. Be an encourager.

2. *Blessings.* In the Bible, fathers traditionally gave purposeful or even ceremonial blessings to their children, often accompanied by inspiring, empowering, or prophetic words. Those specific blessings would stay with that child for life—even for generations. While it may not be as common in the twenty-first century to give blessings to our children, it can have a powerful, long-lasting impact. It certainly did for George and Kyle.

George talks of his father's tremendous influence and the intentional blessings he received from his dad. It's no mistake that George is now a great influence in his own son's life. But Kyle waited forty years to hear his father say, "I love you." Then, when his father was in the hospital after a stroke, he finally did say it. Kyle observed, "I don't think anyone will ever say anything that will mean more to me. It was like a weight had been lifted off my shoulders."

But most of us did not receive words of love and blessing from our own fathers, so even though we may want to give blessings to our children, we don't have a good idea what that looks, sounds, or feels like. I hope to help you fill in some of those blanks.

Keep in mind that blessings can be:

- *Short and spontaneous:* "I love you." "You make me so happy." "I'm so proud to be your dad."

- *Planned and deliberate:* "Brian, you're my son. I love you, and I'll always love you. You are a Jones, from a long line of men who were committed to their families. I am so pleased with you and so proud of you."

- *Given in prayers.* Do this regularly. Imagine what it would have felt like—or think back to what it did feel like—to hear your father pray regular blessings upon your life, your character, and your future. I am not suggesting using prayer to send a message about what you think your child needs to work on, as in *Lord, help Josh to improve his table manners.* Instead, simply praise God for your child and request His blessings on your child's life. For example, you might pray something like this:

Dear Heavenly Father, I thank You tonight for my son Josh. He is such a delight to me, and I am so happy to be his dad. I ask for Your blessing to be on him. He is your child, and I know You have great plans for him. May his eyes always seek Your wisdom and his heart always be sensitive to Your leading. May he love Your Word. As he grows, lead him in Your ways so that he will honor You all his life. Thank You for Josh and how he has brought so much joy to my life. In Christ's name I pray, amen.

- *Taken from God's Word.* I sometimes adapt prayers in the Bible and pray them as blessings over my children. For example, here is a prayer based on Ephesians 3:14–21 NIV:

For this reason I kneel before You, Father, from whom Your whole family in heaven and on earth derives its name. I pray that out of Your glorious riches, You may strengthen Rachel with power through Your Spirit in her inner being so that Christ may dwell in her heart through faith. And I pray that Rachel, being rooted and established in love, may have power, together with all the saints, to grasp how wide

*and long and high and deep is the love of Christ, and to
know this love that surpasses knowledge—that she may be
filled to the measure of all the fullness of God.*

At first, it may seem uncomfortable to bless your children like this,
but there are huge benefits. Recently, after one of our Father-Daughter
Summit events, a girl of about seventeen tearfully told what it meant
to her. She said, "Thank you for this event—because I've had the
chance to hear my father tell me how he feels about me. Every daughter deserves the chance to hear her father say, 'I love you,' and I know
that not very many sons and daughters get to hear that."

Dad, if you've ever thought your words of affirmation and blessing don't make a difference to your children, think again. Even if your
kids shrug off what you say or act embarrassed by it, be assured they're
really soaking it up. As fathers, it's time to make a bold step of faith
and give our children what they deserve.

BE COMMITTED TO THEIR WELL-BEING

When we stay in close contact with our children and make daily efforts to be aware of what's going on in their lives, we're reminding
them over and over again just how important they are to us and how
much we love them. Through our commitment we can communicate
to our children "I want to find out more and more about you, because
you're my child, and you're fascinating. You matter . . . and I love you."

Some of the best fathering stories come from extraordinary situations. I know men who have altered the course of their careers and
their entire lives to take care of their special-needs children—children
facing unusual physical or mental challenges. Those men should inspire us, but we should also recognize that *all* kids, to some extent,
have special needs and will at times require us to make sacrifices. You

may have to sacrifice career advancement, activities you enjoy, or even extra service in your community or church for the sake of your children's welfare. Dads of destiny sometimes have to sacrifice what is *good* for what is *best*.

For example, because you are committed to loving your kids through your actions, you:

- Stay up late to help your son with a speech that he's nervous about—even though you have a presentation to give at work the next day.

- Give up your Saturday round of golf to go bicycle riding with your daughter.

- Get up at 3:30 a.m. to care for a sick child.

- Help with homework.

- Have that hard talk with your teenager.

- Drive your children back and forth to their events.

- Change diapers!

- Show up at your kids' school events.

You're a dad, and these are some of the ways fathers express their love.

In Matthew 6:21 Jesus tells us, "Where your treasure is, there your heart will be also" (NIV). He is talking about heaven, where moth and rust cannot destroy our inheritance (see Matthew 6:19), but I think the principle also applies to things we value here on earth. In other words, the people or things we treasure through our actions are the things that capture our heart. As fathers we're often asked to do things that aren't fun or convenient. The secret to loving our children is not waiting until the feeling arrives and then acting. It's knowing what's right, seeing what your child needs, and doing it. Love is more about commitment and determination than feelings.

Committed dads recognize that difficult circumstances aren't an excuse to bow out on their responsibilities. Fathers father. Growing fathers find ways to be effective, whether in the face of life's busy routine or in the face of adversity and discouragement.

It may seem like no one notices all you do, but the fruit of committed fathering—a close bond with your children—is its own reward. Few things in life are more sweetly satisfying.

MEETING THE CHALLENGE

Showing Love

A father fills the emotional cups of his children and responds to their needs through actions and words that encourage and affirm them.

INSTRUCTIONS:

On a scale of 1 to 5, rank the accuracy of the following statements. Then add your scores and plot your total on the scale below. (You may want to have your child's mother or someone who knows you well take the survey and then compare their answers to yours. If your child no longer lives at home, score yourself as you remember your involvement.)

5 = Mostly True
4 = Somewhat True
3 = Undecided
2 = Somewhat False
1 = Mostly False

1. It is easy for me to encourage my children. ☐

2. When my children are upset, I usually try to listen to them. ☐

3. I constantly tell my children that I love them. ☐

4. I praise my children for things they do well. ☐

5. I point out qualities in my children that I like about them. ☐

6. I tell my children they are special to me. ☐

TOTAL ☐

PLOT YOUR SCORE:

6	18	20	24	27	30
VERY POOR	POOR	AVERAGE	GOOD	VERY GOOD

(The scale is not uniform because it is based on norms from a study of 1,516 fathers.)

QUESTIONS FOR DISCUSSION AND REFLECTION

As you consider how you scored on this inventory, think about the following questions or discuss them with some other fathers.

1. How did your own father and/or mother express their love for you? (e.g., helpful deeds, words of affection, and so on).

2. When was the last time you expressed words of support to your children? Do your children recognize when you are expressing affection?

3. What can you do to become more "approachable" in your children's eyes?

4. What causes you to hesitate in nurturing your children?

5. What qualities would you like to see in your children as they mature? How do your words of encouragement contribute to that?

ACTION POINTS

Choose one of the following action points and commit to doing it before you go on to the next chapter (or your next group meeting).

1. Read, ponder, and then memorize Ephesians 3:14–19.

2. Praise your children for something in front of their friends.

3. Read a book or short story to your children tonight. Include them and yourself in the plot.

4. Put your hand on your children's head, shoulder, or arm as you talk to them.

5. Don't shy away from your teenage daughter; continue to give her appropriate physical signs of affection.

6. Tell your kids, "I need a hug."

7. Buy five or ten postcards for each child, and on each one write how much you love him or her and one hope you have for his or her life. Mail them over the next month or so.

8. Tell your children what special qualities you see in them.

9. Ask your daughter what she likes to do with you, and set a date to do that together.

10. At the dinner table, tell each child one quality that you appreciate in him or her.

CHAPTER 3

EXTEND GRACE AND
FORGIVENESS

Bear with each other and forgive whatever
grievances you may have against one another.
Forgive as the Lord forgave you.

CoLOSSIANS 3:13 NIV

Golf legend Chi Chi Rodriguez first learned about grace and forgiveness from his father. Rodriguez says, "When I was a boy we were so poor, the biggest present I ever got was a marble. But we were rich in other ways, and my father was my hero."

One day, Chi Chi's father caught one of the neighborhood boys stealing bananas from a tree in their yard. He sent the boy home, but he knew that some other action was necessary. He also knew that this was a great time to be a model for his son. So he told Chi Chi to go get the machete. Now, you can imagine what kinds of thoughts stirred in this young boy's mind. Something horrible was going to happen.

But instead, something marvelous happened. Chi Chi's father climbed the tree, cut down some bananas, then took Chi Chi with him to deliver them to the boy and his family. Chi Chi says that this powerful demonstration of mercy and forgiveness has stayed with him all these years.

We fathers are concerned with teaching our children about honesty, integrity, and respecting others. When our children mess up, we want to make sure they understand and learn from the consequences of their actions. While those principles must be taught, too often fathers model justice by being rigid and legalistic. Dads of destiny must purposefully balance this by modeling fatherly grace and mercy in visible, powerful ways.

THE POWER OF FORGIVENESS

Forgiveness can sound so simple. But, of course, it isn't. Forgiveness is more than just mumbling "Please forgive me" or "You're forgiven." Forgiveness is a *decision,* an *act of will.* One *chooses* to forgive or not forgive. It is a decisive and deliberate choice to forgive someone who has sinned against you. Forgiveness is powerful because it is a source of healing, and when it's given and experienced, relationships can be incredibly transformed.

The following story powerfully illustrates this truth.

Del was a Christian husband and father of two who found himself faced with the huge challenge of forgiving his wife after she had left him for another man. A pastoral counselor helped Del think through the problems in his marriage and eventually brought up the idea of forgiving his wife for leaving him. At the time, forgiving her seemed unthinkable. But after several months, Del found the strength to begin praying for her. Eventually, he chose to forgive his wife and the man who shared in her unfaithfulness, and he began to feel a freedom from his bitterness.

Over a year later, Del received a phone call from his wife (they had never divorced), asking if she could come back home and assuring him that she wanted to work on their marriage. Now

Del was faced with living out his valiant act of forgiveness. It was a slow, cautious process, but he agreed to let his wife come home.

Three years later, the couple had another child, a beautiful daughter who brought them great joy. Not long after the birth of their daughter, Del's wife was diagnosed with cancer, and she died a few years later. Del treasured all his children and did his best to raise three responsible, godly people.

The youngest daughter grew up, married, and had a son, who is now a teenager. Recently, Del's grandson told him, "Grandpa, I'm a miracle. You forgave my grandma and so my mom was born. You took care of her, and now I'm here. Thanks, Grandpa, for being a miracle for me." You can be sure this grandson will encourage his own children to be forgiving of others who have hurt them. The mercy Del showed toward his wife has become a rich, enduring legacy of forgiveness that his family will cherish for generations.

When relationships are mended after times of great turmoil, it's evidence of a holy God overcoming evil. The results are supernatural when we imitate the Father by extending grace and forgiveness.

HOW THE HEAVENLY FATHER FORGIVES US

The parable of the prodigal son in Luke 15 is one of the best short stories ever recorded. It illustrates a father extending grace and forgiveness to both of his sons. You know what happens. The younger son asks for his inheritance, leaves home, and blows all his money, while the older son compliantly serves his father. Eventually, the younger son, broke and hungry, heads home to be a servant in his father's house.

We can imagine the father, sitting on the porch, scanning the horizon every day for months or years—hoping his son will return. When he finally sees his son, there's no "I told you so" or "I hope you learned your lesson, young man." Instead the father runs to greet him, throws his arms around him, and kisses him. The son, in his brokenness, confesses to the father the error of his ways and that he is no longer worthy to be called his son.

The father receives his son's confession but quickly brings a robe, a ring, and shoes and escorts him to a lavish celebration to demonstrate to all that he has forgiven his son. Meanwhile, the older son becomes angry and jealous, so the father takes the initiative to reach out to him. The father doesn't belittle the older son but assures him with affection that he has access to the same grace and mercy shown to his brother, along with everything else the father owns.

> To err is human, to forgive divine.
> ALEXANDER POPE

The power of this parable revolves around the actions of the father. Whether the reader identifies more closely with the risk-taking, pleasure-bent younger son or the hard-working, compliant older brother is of little consequence. The overriding theme is that in the father's house, there is sufficient love to accommodate both of them. If the sons choose to receive their father's love, their capacity to love will grow and become the basis for outloving their world.

Elsewhere in Scripture, we're told that when God forgives His children, He doesn't hold the offense against them. He doesn't keep throwing it in our face, reminding us over and over again of our sin. Read and meditate on these passages:

Blessed is the one whose transgression is forgiven, whose sin is covered. Blessed is the man against whom the LORD counts no iniquity, and in whose spirit there is no deceit. (Psalm 32:1–2)

For you, O LORD, are good and forgiving, abounding in steadfast love to all who call upon you. Give ear, O LORD, to my prayer; listen to my plea for grace. In the day of my trouble I call upon you, for you answer me. (Psalm 86:5–7)

For as high as the heavens are above the earth, so great is his steadfast love toward those who fear him; as far as the east is from the west, so far does he remove our transgressions from us. (Psalm 103:11–12)

Human error and divine forgiveness are central features to God's message on earth. And since God expressed Himself as a heavenly *Father*, we can make some meaningful applications in regard to our own fathering. How can we teach our children to outlove the world through forgiveness? Again, a large portion of it rests on our modeling. Have we forgiven those who have wronged us? Is our daily speech seasoned with grace toward others? Are our children learning about the biblical concepts of forgiveness and mercy? If we want to teach our kids to extend grace and forgiveness and thereby outlove the world, we need to give them a clean slate, initiate forgiveness, and seek their forgiveness when we've wronged them.

GIVE THEM A CLEAN SLATE

Just as the heavenly Father doesn't hold our offenses against us, neither should we earthly fathers hold our children's offenses against them. No one wants to be reminded of shortcomings—including our kids. Wise is the father who follows his heavenly Father's example in this.

One committed dad wrote this about how he intentionally teaches his children about God's forgiveness and grace:

When our second child was young, she did something she should not have done. Since she was a very sensitive child and I did not want to prolong the punishment, I chose to spank her. But also, again because she was so sensitive, I took positive, immediate action to restore our relationship. After the spanking—not a harsh one, mind you!—I gathered her into my arms, dried her tears, and said this: "Amy, what you did was wrong. I had to punish you because I love you, and I have to teach you how to do what is right. I know you're sorry. And God knows you're sorry. God forgives you and I forgive you, too. Now, this is very important: So you know that I really do forgive you, I promise to never, ever mention this again."

Then I had to keep that promise. I didn't report the incident to my wife. I didn't bring it up again the next time there was a problem. In fact, if I wanted to tell you now what it was, I wouldn't be able to, because I've totally forgotten it.

And so has Amy. But she has not forgotten that her father loves her enough to forget what is forgiven. And she knows how that is done.

It's a principle modeled by our perfect heavenly Father and one we fallible human fathers can emulate. It gives our children the clean slate they need in order to do better the next time. It affirms our trust in them. And it makes us practice what we preach. For who would ever want to break that kind of promise to a tender little girl?

When a dad forgives his child and proclaims that forgiveness—not as a source of pride, but out of concern for a restored relationship—he is showing the child through his example the liberating power of forgiveness.

In Matthew 18 Jesus tells a parable about a servant who is forgiven a great debt but is then unwilling to forgive a small debt owed to him. Jesus's point is clear: We cannot experience forgiveness if we are unwilling to forgive those who sin against us. When we don't forgive someone, it binds that individual to us in a similar way that a debt binds us to the one to whom we owe money. When we forgive, we release the person's feelings of guilt and tension. What loving father would deny his children of such a gift?

TAKE THE INITIATIVE

A father once asked me to pray for him and his teenage son. He said they were "always at each others' throats" and nothing he had tried seemed to work. I suspect that what that dad really needed was to ask for—and extend—some forgiveness toward his son. Imagine how powerful an exchange like that would be in that home!

When it comes to forgiveness, we fathers must take the initiative. Our example of forgiveness teaches our children a valuable life skill that will strengthen their relationships—and we pass on awesome lessons about God's grace. Our children's concepts of God—and their ability to depend on God—begin with how we, as their earthly fathers, relate to them.

I'm convinced that one of the secrets and great strengths of the kingdom of God is being able to receive and grant forgiveness. We all sin, and often that leaves a trail of damaged relationships, maybe between us and another person, and always between us and God. Loving fathers are committed to granting their children grace and forgiveness, just as we hope they'll do for others, including us when we criticize them harshly, place other priorities ahead of them, or fail to affirm them.

SEEK THEIR FORGIVENESS

I can vividly remember a time when I needed to seek forgiveness as a father. It was a hot summer day, and good ol' Dad was called in to resolve another family dispute. "Joel, tell me the truth!"

My son looked at me indignantly.

"Joel, are you telling the truth?"

"Yes, Dad. Honest."

I knew that if I studied his face long enough, he'd give himself away. But that day, he was rock solid. So . . . I made the call. "No, you're not, Joel. I don't believe you."

As I doled out the appropriate punishment, Joel showed no sign of remorse. Minutes later, I found out through one of the other kids that Joel had been telling the truth. I had judged him and punished him unfairly. I was wrong.

So I went to Joel and said, "Son, you were right. I was wrong. You were telling the truth, and I am sorry I didn't believe you. It was my mistake. Will you forgive me?"

Joel smiled, said, "Yeah, Dad," and went happily on his way.

I don't think there's anything more challenging for a father than coming face-to-face with his own mistakes. You know what you have to do: go back to the child, confess that you were wrong, and ask for forgiveness. It's humbling, to be sure, but it's also one of the most important things you can do as a father. It's the ultimate moment of modeling.

Asking your children for forgiveness demonstrates that, as in all relationships, there is give-and-take. It shows them that your rules of discipline are not arbitrary and that you hold yourself accountable to those rules as well. When you admit you were wrong and seek their forgiveness, you prove to your children that restoring the trust of the relationship is more important than your own pride.

But it goes even further. Think of the relief your children must feel when you own up to your mistakes. When you punish your children unjustly, instead of simply blowing off what you've done or saying "Hey life isn't fair," be responsive to their feelings and try to make things right. By doing this, you will make them feel valuable and loved.

Have you blown it recently? Do you need to go back to your child and make things right?

We all make mistakes that hurt the people around us—including our children. And we all need forgiveness. We can commit our lives to our kids, demonstrate love, and model integrity. But when we are willing to set aside our egos, be vulnerable, say we were wrong, and ask their forgiveness, that's when our children know we really mean what we teach. Asking for forgiveness is one of the most courageous things we can do.

What's more, it gives our children opportunities to forgive. Of course, we don't want to start making mistakes as a father so we can teach our children to forgive. But as dads we do inevitably fail, and when we do, we need to practice humility as much as our kids need to practice forgiveness, because forgiveness enables them to let go and move on.

LETTING GO AND MOVING ON

Several years ago, I had the opportunity to meet with twelve young men at an inner-city school. When I asked about their fathers, eleven of the twelve described them with negative words: "He was never there." "He's a deadbeat." "Useless." "He's a sorry lowlife." "Loser." "He just up and left us." "He don't do nothing." Almost half of the students used profanity, and the only description that wasn't negative was "He was hard working."

Then I pushed it a step further. I challenged them to take action and forgive their fathers. I told them that although they had no control over what their fathers did or didn't do, they all had control over their response to their fathers' lives. But as soon as I said, "Forgive your father," the mood of the room turned tense. All but one of the students reacted with comments such as "I ain't never going to forgive that man." "There's no way I'd do that." "I'll never forgive." The only exception was a young man who said this to the group: "Now you guys know me and you know who my father is; you know my situation. But I want you to know, I've forgiven him and put the past behind me. Why don't you all think about letting go and moving on?"

This young man has grasped an important truth about forgiveness that all of us—fathers and children alike—need to learn: forgiving others is good for us, even when the person we're forgiving isn't interested in restoring the relationship. People will always let us down; this is an inevitable reality of the world. But if we can teach our children to exercise forgiveness, we can be sure that they will outlove the world.

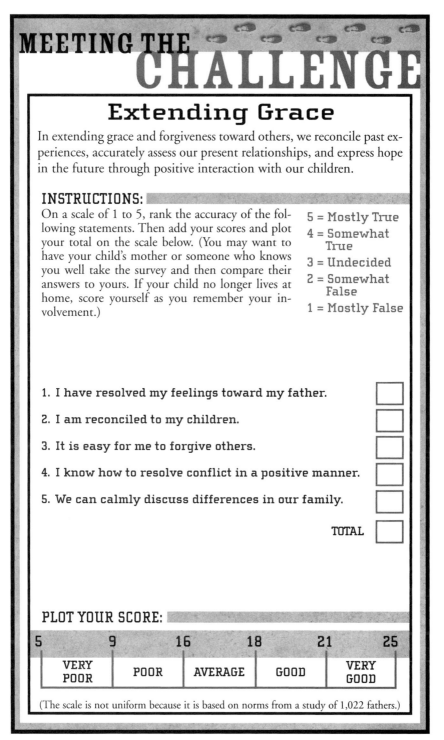

MEETING THE CHALLENGE

Extending Grace

In extending grace and forgiveness toward others, we reconcile past experiences, accurately assess our present relationships, and express hope in the future through positive interaction with our children.

INSTRUCTIONS:

On a scale of 1 to 5, rank the accuracy of the following statements. Then add your scores and plot your total on the scale below. (You may want to have your child's mother or someone who knows you well take the survey and then compare their answers to yours. If your child no longer lives at home, score yourself as you remember your involvement.)

5 = Mostly True
4 = Somewhat True
3 = Undecided
2 = Somewhat False
1 = Mostly False

1. I have resolved my feelings toward my father. ☐

2. I am reconciled to my children. ☐

3. It is easy for me to forgive others. ☐

4. I know how to resolve conflict in a positive manner. ☐

5. We can calmly discuss differences in our family. ☐

TOTAL ☐

PLOT YOUR SCORE:

5	9	16	18	21	25
VERY POOR	POOR	AVERAGE	GOOD	VERY GOOD

(The scale is not uniform because it is based on norms from a study of 1,022 fathers.)

QUESTIONS FOR DISCUSSION AND REFLECTION

As you consider how you scored on this inventory, think about the following questions or discuss them with some other fathers.

1. How were conflicts handled in your household when you were a child?

2. Do you have unresolved conflicts or feelings toward your father or someone else in your family? If so, what action can you take to bring about a resolution?

3. When was the last time you went to your child to ask forgiveness for some wrong you had done? What was the result, and what did you learn for next time?

4. What does it mean to forgive? Is it a feeling or a decision? Does it remove the consequences of the wrong that has been done?

ACTION POINTS

Choose one of the following action points and commit to doing it before you go on to the next chapter (or your next group meeting).

1. Read the parable in Luke 15 and with another father discuss which of the two sons in the story you most identify with, and why.

2. Look for opportunities to extend grace that are far better than what your kids' actions deserve.

3. Regularly check in with your children about challenges in relationships they are facing at school or elsewhere. Just listen and encourage and seek to be more understanding as you relate to them.

4. Talk to your children about how they can resolve conflict, using examples from your own past. Talk about the times you successfully dealt with conflict and the times you fell short.

5. Get to know your children's friends; make it your mission to listen to them and find their positive qualities. You'll be better equipped to help them when conflicts arise.

6. With minor, everyday sibling disagreements, encourage your children and express confidence that they can work out a solution on their own.

7. After one of your children has a tantrum or conflict, seek to build a closer relationship through healing words, touches, and blessings.

8. Reach out to the parents of a child with whom your son or daughter has a conflict.

9. Brainstorm or role-play with your children about a variety of situations that are tense or difficult. Help them think through healthy, grace-filled responses. Establish healthy household rules for dealing with conflict: staying calm, listening, avoiding defensive language, respecting others' opinions, not arguing about things said in the past, and so on.

10. Consistently pray that God would give your children a keen sense of His forgiveness and grace in their lives.

CHAPTER 4

HELP THEM REACH OUT TO OTHERS

As you sent me into the world, so I have sent them into the world.

JOHN 17:18

In his best-selling book, *The Purpose-Driven Life,* Rick Warren challenges fathers to give their children "focused attention." By his definition, focused attention involves concentrating "so intently on your child that you forget about yourself at the moment."[1] In essence, what you're saying to your child is, "I value you enough to give you my most precious asset, my time." Warren continues, "Whenever you give your time, you are making a sacrifice, and sacrifice is the essence of love."[2] Warren's book is a forty-day spiritual journey that challenges readers to wrestle with one of life's most important questions: "What on earth am I here for?"

Rick Warren himself is a product of healthy fathering. His father, who died of cancer in 1999, served as a pastor for more than fifty years. In the book, Warren describes the scene in the hospital during the final week of his dad's life. His father was almost always semiconscious and would talk aloud as he dreamed. Warren writes, "As I sat by his bed with tears flowing down my cheeks, I bowed my head to thank God for my dad's faith. At that moment Dad reached out and placed his frail hand on my head . . . as if commissioning me. . . . 'Save one more for Jesus! Save one more for Jesus!'"[3]

Warren says his father's words that night became the focal theme for the rest of his life, and his life demonstrates the fruit of that commitment. He pastors Saddleback Community Church in Southern California, with a weekly attendance of more than twenty thousand. His purpose-driven materials have been read by millions and are full of challenges to live "an examined life," rooted in service to others.

As Rick Warren's life demonstrates, when we dads set the example of service to God, our children will be more likely to follow. What might a powerful example of authentic faith involve for you? How can you model reaching out to others? Maybe it's by reaching out to orphans and widows or to the homeless or fatherless in your community. Maybe it's reaching out to a neighbor who's going through a difficult time or inviting your son's new classmate over to play. Maybe it is as simple as inviting others into your home.

SHOW HOSPITALITY

In a hot, rugged desert, Abraham gave a gracious reception to three men he didn't know (see Genesis 18). Abraham attended to his guests' immediate needs, asking for water to be brought so they could wash their feet and feeding them a lavish meal. He bowed low to the ground, a common greeting in the Middle East. He spoke to them respectfully, as if he were their servant. In the ancient world, hospitality was a responsibility of the heads of households.

Perhaps you have always left hospitality to your wife because she is the "people person" in your family. Or maybe she's the better cook or more comfortable with having people over for dinner. Fine, but that doesn't let you off the hook. You can learn and grow in this area. God instructed—and Jesus repeated—"Love the Lord your God with all your heart and with all your soul and with all your mind" and "Love your neighbor as yourself" (Matthew 22:37, 39). For, "Whatever you did for one of the least of these brothers of mine, you did for me" (Matthew 25:40 NIV).

When we obey these commandments by opening up our homes, we create lasting memories for our children to cherish, and we nurture a habit that will likely carry over into their adult lives.

Dads, we need to be the instigators of hospitality. We can show hospitality by:

- Giving our neighbors an open invitation to ask us for help in emergencies.
- Helping other families with yard work.
- Taking meals to brand-new parents or someone who is ill.
- Including every child in neighborhood games.
- Hosting missionaries on furlough.
- Inviting a neighbor kid on your family outing.
- Having people over for dinner—often.

Make your home a place of hospitality, and then extend that hospitality outward by involving your children in acts of service.

INVOLVE YOUR KIDS IN ACTS OF SERVICE

While many dads understand the need for family devotions and for praying with their kids and going to church, they don't often think about how they can involve their children in their serving others. Yet active service is at the heart of true religion. James 1:27 says, "Religion that God our Father accepts as pure and faultless is this: to look after orphans and widows in their distress and to keep oneself from being polluted by the world" (NIV).

When we model service to others, we give our children real-life experiences to see faith in action. Dad, your kids need to see you serving others willingly and joyfully—and they need to be involved with you.

Here are some ideas for how your family can team up to serve others:

- As a family prepare a shoebox of supplies to send overseas to a missionary or needy family.

- Join your younger children in making a card to send to a shut-in or someone in the nursing home.

- Invite a single dad and his kids over for dinner.

- Rake leaves or shovel the walk of an elderly neighbor.

- Change the oil or complete some maintenance on the car of a single mom who lives on your street.

- Bring food to several families in an inner-city project.

- Go as a family on your church's mission trip.

Show your children that serving others is a way of life—as it should be for every authentic Christian. Prove to them that your faith isn't dead, because it naturally leads to deeds. If you really believe God is at work in the world around you, be part of that work. And if you are, your kids will see God working in the lives of others and in your life.

DISCUSS WHAT GOD SAYS ABOUT HELPING OTHERS

The Bible has much to say about the importance of serving others. For example:

- Galatians 5:13 tells us that we were called to be free, but instead of using our freedom to sin, we should serve one another in love.

- Ephesians 4:32 says, "Be kind and compassionate to one another, forgiving each other" (NIV).

- Ephesians 6:7 urges us to "serve wholeheartedly," as if we are serving the Lord instead of men.

- In Matthew 25:40, Jesus says that when we feed, clothe, and care for "the least of these," we are also doing those things for Him.

Several years ago, our family was studying the book of James. In chapter 2, it says, "Suppose a brother or sister is without clothes and daily food. If one of you says to him, 'Go, I wish you well; keep warm and well fed,' but does nothing about his physical needs, what good is it? In the same way, faith by itself, if it is not accompanied by action, is dead" (vv. 15–17 NIV).

As we talked about what those verses mean and who we might know who was without food or clothing, my children thought of Skip, a man they had grown acquainted with who was unemployed because of a medical condition. We talked about what we might do to help this man, and since it was close to Christmas, we decided to bring Christmas to Skip's house, out of obedience to what God was telling us as a family.

One of my sons recently came across Galatians 6:10, which says: "Therefore, as we have opportunity, let us do good to all people, especially to those who belong to the family of believers" (NIV). He and I memorized that verse together, and then, wouldn't you know it, three days later, out of the goodness of his heart—no, out of the inspiration of the scripture he'd memorized—my son took treats to school with no apparent purpose other than to bless his fellow classmates.

God's Word helps our kids see life from God's perspective. It also reminds us about the character traits, virtues, and acts of service we can encourage and plant in them. As fathers we're called to help cultivate the fruit God wants to bear in the world *through our kids.*

ENCOURAGE INTENTIONAL ACTS OF KINDNESS

We can also help encourage our kids to do intentional acts of kindness by teaching them to see a need and respond to it. Here's an example: Let's say you live in an area of the country where it snows, and when it does, your driveway needs to be shoveled. Rather than waiting until the night it snows to try to recruit some help, plant the idea in your son's head well before it snows, and see if he picks up on it. If he doesn't, be patient and just keep planting the seed. It may just take more time. But if he does shovel the driveway, give him all kinds of positive reinforcement.

You can help your kids develop sensitivity for a friend who's been left out, a needy neighbor, or a family member who's struggling by asking, "Who seems really troubled right now? What can we do to help or encourage him?" Or, "How can we make her life a little easier?" Try to create the impression that kindness and thoughtfulness are natural responses, and reward your children when they take initiative.

It doesn't always take a lot of effort on our part to get our kids to reach out. They often see possible ways to do good that we don't notice. They can take simple ideas and run with them to create something amazing. Just plant the seed, Dad, and allow another Father to water it. Here are three examples of what happens when dads do just that.

- Every week for several months Robert would read his children a story about the courageous work of World Impact, an urban outreach to America's poorest. One night Robert's son was so moved by the stories of sacrificial service that he gathered all the money in his possession and presented it to his father with a note, which read, "Dad, get this money to the World Impact leaders. We have to help them."

- Annie and Rebecca, who are in their teens, both have birthdays in late October. One year they decided to combine their birthday parties into one big event. But they wanted to do something different. So they asked their friends to bring *not* birthday presents, but children's Christmas gifts or money. About sixty kids showed up and had a great time at the party. But even better was the good that resulted. The group brought together about fifty toys and $350. That December, Annie and Rebecca helped to distribute the gifts and money to needy children through an inner-city organization that helps struggling families.

The Empathy Factor
Several studies have noted the fact that when fathers were involved in their children's lives, the empathy scores of those children were significantly higher. In other words, if you are involved in your children's lives and help them consider ways to creatively reach out to others, they will in turn have more empathy for others in need.[4]

Annie's father encouraged this outreach and then provided the logistical support to get all the gifts delivered.

- Adam's father would regularly update his family about the health of Sarah Jones, who was dying of cancer. Sarah had four children who were struggling with the pain of losing their mother. Sarah's oldest child, Mike, was absorbing the brunt of the family grief, as well as cooking the meals, cleaning the house, and helping his younger siblings with their homework. One evening Adam decided to kidnap Mike and drive him to a small get-together in his honor. It was their simple way of saying to Mike, "We realize things have been hard for you, and we know Christmas will be difficult too. We want you to know that we're here for you."

Dad, we need to be about these things too.

HELP THEM TRANSFORM THE WORLD

We want our children to be about God's business, whether they are missionaries or pastors, teachers or engineers, stay-at-home moms or entrepreneurs. We don't just want them to make the world a *better* place; we want them to help transform it by God's power working in them. We need to proclaim with our lives that we aren't here just to be served or to take up space; we're here to make a difference for Christ by outloving the world. If we can convey that message convincingly to our children, we will exponentially expand our influence to future generations.

I'll end this chapter with one of my favorite stories about how parents can teach their children to care for others, which was sent to me a few years ago. I hope you find it as inspiring as I do.

Just a small, white envelope stuck among the branches of our

Christmas tree. No name, no identification, no inscription. It has peeked through the branches of our tree for the past ten years or so.

The tradition began because my husband, Mike, hated the commercial aspects of Christmas: overspending, the last-minute running around to get a tie for Uncle Harry and the dusting powder for Grandma—gifts given in desperation because you couldn't think of anything else. So one year I bypassed the usual shirts, sweaters, and ties, and I reached for something special, just for Mike. The inspiration came in an unusual way.

Our son Kevin, who was twelve that year, had a wrestling match shortly before Christmas—a nonleague match against a team sponsored by an inner-city church. These youngsters, dressed in ragged sneakers, presented a sharp contrast to our boys in their spiffy blue and gold uniforms and sparkling new wrestling shoes. I was alarmed to see that the other team was wrestling with no headgear to protect their ears—a luxury they obviously could not afford. We ended up walloping them. We took every weight class. And as each of their boys got up from the mat, he swaggered around with false bravado, a kind of street pride that couldn't acknowledge defeat. Mike, seated beside me, shook his head sadly. "I wish just one of them could have won," he said. "They have a lot of potential, but losing like this could take the heart right out of them." Mike always loved kids—all kids.

That's when I got the idea. That afternoon, I went to a sporting-goods store and bought an assortment of wrestling headgear and shoes and sent them anonymously to the inner-city church. On Christmas Eve, I placed the envelope on the tree with a note inside, telling Mike what I had done as my gift to him. His smile was the brightest thing about Christmas that year and in succeeding years. For each Christmas, I followed the tradition—one year sending a group of mentally disabled youngsters to a hockey game, another year a check to a pair of elderly brothers whose home had burned to the ground the week before Christmas, and on and on.

The envelope became the highlight of our Christmas. It was always the last gift opened, and our children, ignoring their new toys, would stand with wide-eyed anticipation as their dad lifted the envelope from the tree to reveal its contents. As the children grew, the envelope never lost its allure.

The story doesn't end there. You see, we lost Mike last year due to dreaded cancer. When Christmas rolled around, I was still so wrapped in grief that I barely got the tree up. But Christmas Eve found me placing an envelope on the tree, and in the morning, it was joined by three more.

Each of our children, unknown to the others, had placed an envelope on the tree for their dad. The tradition has grown and someday will expand even further with our grandchildren standing around the tree with wide-eyed anticipation watching as their fathers take down the envelope. Mike's spirit, like the Christmas spirit, will always be with us.

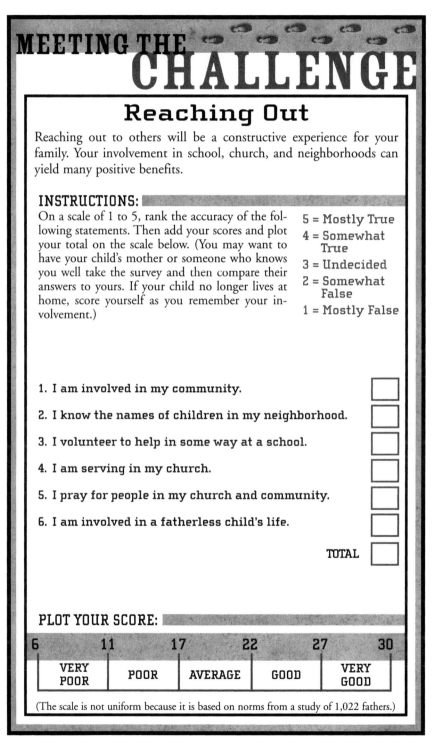

MEETING THE CHALLENGE

Reaching Out

Reaching out to others will be a constructive experience for your family. Your involvement in school, church, and neighborhoods can yield many positive benefits.

INSTRUCTIONS:

On a scale of 1 to 5, rank the accuracy of the following statements. Then add your scores and plot your total on the scale below. (You may want to have your child's mother or someone who knows you well take the survey and then compare their answers to yours. If your child no longer lives at home, score yourself as you remember your involvement.)

5 = Mostly True
4 = Somewhat True
3 = Undecided
2 = Somewhat False
1 = Mostly False

1. I am involved in my community.

2. I know the names of children in my neighborhood.

3. I volunteer to help in some way at a school.

4. I am serving in my church.

5. I pray for people in my church and community.

6. I am involved in a fatherless child's life.

TOTAL

PLOT YOUR SCORE:

6	11	17	22	27	30
VERY POOR	POOR	AVERAGE	GOOD	VERY GOOD

(The scale is not uniform because it is based on norms from a study of 1,022 fathers.)

QUESTIONS FOR DISCUSSION AND REFLECTION

As you consider how you scored on this inventory, think about the following questions or discuss them with some other fathers.

1. While you were growing up, did your family reach out to others?

2. What percent of your time is used in helping others outside of your own family?

3. Are you involved in any efforts to reach out to those with pressing needs?

4. Discuss successful programs that provide safe and healthy places for children to gather. What makes them effective? How can your local church initiate or contribute to an existing outreach?

ACTION POINTS

Choose one of the following action points and commit to doing it before you go on to the next chapter (or your next group meeting).

1. Make a hospital visit or stop by to see a shut-in. Take your children along as a team effort to reach out to them.

2. Ask your children if they know of anyone in your neighborhood who needs help. Plan a day where your family can perform some simple acts of service to help them.

3. Tell your children a story of someone who reached out to you when you were young and how that made a difference.

4. Discuss the family budget, focusing on how you share your resources with the poor and support worthy causes.

5. Plan a short-term missions experience with your family, one that involves your serving together.

6. Construct or add to your family mission statement for the coming year. As a family determine whom you are going to help.

7. Discuss ways you plan to care for your extended family.

8. Invite neighbors over for a dinner or plan a block party.

PART TWO

Outthinking the World

Dads of destiny are called upon to live above the world in every way, including the way they think. The apostle Paul, though not a natural father, taught his spiritual children how to *outthink* the world by admonishing them to fix their minds on things above—things that are rooted in God's truth. Outthinking the world includes taking an active role in our children's education and teaching them how to temper their learning with faith and love. As fathers become dynamically involved in their children's education, they model lifelong learning and a willingness to help their children gain knowledge and wisdom, yielding a discerning mind that will be filled with vision and revelation.

CHAPTER 5

TEACH DISCERNMENT

Be transformed by the renewal of your mind,
that by testing you may discern what is the will
of God.

ROMANS 12:2

For children, who are discovering the world for the first time, every-thing is new. As they mature they will begin to explore their belief sys-tem and try to discern the deeper questions of life: *Why am I here? Is there a God? How can I know Him?*

Jeremiah 6:16 says, "Stand at the crossroads and look; ask for the ancient paths, ask where the good way is, and walk in it" (NIV). No matter how old we are, to our children we are "the ancient paths" of wisdom, and they need the benefit of our experience and wisdom as they consider options and think through possible consequences of their choices. Kids today are under a lot of pressure to look, act, and be a certain way. They need our solid, reliable guidance for how to dis-cern what's right in the midst of all the gray areas in our culture.

If we can teach our children to be discerning—able to distinguish between good and evil, between humility and arrogance—we will sleep soundly at night. But if we are going to succeed in this endeavor,

81

we need to pray King Solomon's prayer: "Give your servant a discerning heart to govern your people and to distinguish between right and wrong" (1 Kings 3:9 NIV).

Sadly, many children do not learn this essential life skill. Consequently they fail to recognize any moral or spiritual absolutes, and many of them drift into the twilight of relativism. That's what happened to Mike Buie. I recently reviewed his profound and unpublished manuscript, *Memoirs of Hate and Pain,* which he wrote during a three-year stint in solitary confinement. His writing chronicles the agony and anguish of being caught in the system and feeling helpless. He draws strong connections between his personal pain, his family's devastation, and his lack of a father to teach him about the world.

Mike came from a family of ten children. He writes, "At one time, there were six of my family members locked away; now there are five of us locked up. Between myself, three brothers, and two sisters, we have given America's prisons nearly 100 years of our lives." Mike served eleven years in prison. He goes on to pinpoint the events and dynamics that led to his family's demise:

> Dad and mom divorced and everything started to crumble. First the dog got shot and killed, and the rats and roaches showed up by the hundreds. Sisters got pregnant and ran away, dropped out of school and went to prison. Mom did the best she could, but children need their father. . . . It has taken me years to get over it, and even now I cringe when I think about what could have been.

Mike is not alone. The penal system is full of men who didn't have a father while growing up and who cringe when they think of what could have been. To develop in a healthy way, young men, in particular, must have an anchor, a role model, a hero. If that role model is their father, their chances of thriving are even better. A dad of destiny provides his children with a solid reference point, which is essential for problem solving and resisting peer pressure.

Discernment is about making wise decisions about life's choices. It's about sifting through opinion, facts, and knowledge, and then judging and examining that information so that you can form a conclusion. As dads it's our job to model discernment and then equip our kids to be discerning as they face tough choices. In this chapter I'd like to talk about some specific things you can do to help your kids develop discernment.

PLANT AND WATER THE SEED OF GOD'S WORD

Discernment needs both seed and soil to germinate and grow. The soil is your child's heart. Children are gifts from God, fashioned in His image. They have the capacity to learn to distinguish between truth and error. If we sow the seed of God's Word in the soil of our children's hearts and then nurture it, it will grow into a fruitful harvest.

Discernment has its origins in what has been called *the natural law* and is best expressed by the Ten Commandments. God gave us these commandments as a foundation for discernment. Indeed, all of God's Word is an optimum source of wisdom and a reference point for truth. The more often we consult the Bible and use it in

> In this democracy, we need to continue to ask for discernment. We are living in a rapidly changing age. The moral climate surrounding our children and our children's children is not like the temptations or wickedness which surrounded us who are a bit older. We need to ask for discernment for ourselves, and we need to ask God how we can speak to the next generation in a way which can be understood.[1]
>
> EDITH SCHAEFFER

the day-to-day routine of family life, the more likely it is that our children will learn to be discerning.

This prompts a few simple questions: Do you have a framed copy of the Ten Commandments in your home? Do your children know the Ten Commandments well enough to know how they apply to their lives? Do you?

Dad, we cannot rely on others to teach discernment to our children. Decades ago, with a federal mandate, the Ten Commandments were taken off the walls of our public classrooms. This fateful act only heightened the need for dads to take leadership in giving their children guidance in the home. We are the planters and gardeners in shaping discernment, and we must use our influence to sew the seeds of biblical truth in our children's hearts. We can make a difference in their lives. But if we fail to plant the seed or neglect to water or feed these truths, our children will not harvest the fruit of a discerning mind and heart.

The process of developing discernment, much like the process of plant development, is a mystery. An agronomist can tell you all the facts surrounding the planting process, but if you press him for the specifics about how plants grow, he will be a little more humble. "We really don't know what triggers life," he might say. "We can describe it, cultivate it, and increase our chances for a maximum yield, but there's a sense of mystery behind growth. There are conditions that we cannot control." The same is true when fathers plant the seeds of discernment. But when we teach our children biblical principles and show them how they apply to daily life, we significantly increase the likelihood that they will grow up to be discerning men and women. (See the next chapter for some specific ideas for how to plant God's Word in the hearts of your children.)

EXPLORE CONSEQUENCES

In addition to planting God's Word in their hearts, you must also help them understand that their actions have consequences, some good and some bad.

As you have heard, positive reinforcement can be a powerful motivator for good behavior. When your child performs a task that makes you proud, acknowledge that child. For example, you can praise a young child's mastery of the social graces, such as saying "thank you," "yes, sir," "no, ma'am," "please," "no, thank you," and so on. As the child matures, you can praise him when he rises when his elders enter the room, opens doors for others, yields his seat or place to a handicapped or needy person. The more you reward the behavior you want to encourage in your kids, the sooner they will learn the benefits of that good behavior.

Along the way you must allow them to experience the consequences of negative behavior and teach them to be wiser about their behavior and choices. However, all children are unique, and some always push the boundaries—even if there is a degree of danger and despite their parents' warning. I have an adage for kids who constantly push the edge, "If the only way they learn is to burn, have ointment ready for when they return."

I am not suggesting that you let your children be exposed to danger without any warning or instruction about what may happen to them as a result. That is unacceptable. Dads of destiny must teach their kids about negative consequences. We see this teaching pattern in Scripture. A good portion of the Old Testament reminds us of the consequences we will suffer if we fail to obey God's commands or trust His promises. The nation of Israel and her kings were constantly having to learn, relearn—and in some cases unlearn—what they should be doing. Some children can be told, reminded, and told again not to touch a hot stove burner, but they disregard the instructions and have to be rushed to the emergency room to get treatment for their burned fingers. While it's tough to see our children get burned by their poor choices, it is better to allow them to fail while they are still living under our care than when they're far away.

In their popular book *Parenting with Love and Logic*, coauthors Jim Fay and Foster Cline encourage parents to allow children to learn from their mistakes while they're young and the consequences are harmless. Lessons learned early help kids develop discernment and pave the way for better decisions down the road, when the consequences are more significant. The following illustration from the book offers parents some unique insight into how children can learn from consequences.

The principal of a junior high called Jim because some of the girls had been putting lip prints all over the bathroom mirrors and walls of school. Nothing he'd done to stop them had worked. First he called an all-school assembly in which he threatened the offending students. Then he wrote letters to parents—again, no change. He talked to the student council and even organized a student SWAT team. Still, the girls kept kissing the mirrors.

So he called Jim to see if he could help. Jim agreed to come, but he didn't have any answers. He was standing in the hallway, talking to the principal, when a woman walked by and overheard their conversation. They explained the problem, and she said, "Oh, sure. I can solve that one. When's the first recess?"

She was a new custodian, and it was her first day on the job. At 10:15, she entered the girls' restroom. Several girls were lining up in front of the mirrors. The custodian carried only two tools: a swab and a squeegee. In dramatic fashion, she went over to one of the toilets, submerged the swab, dripped water across the floor on the way to the sink, and scrubbed those mirrors top to bottom, wiping them "clean." The girls looked at her, amazed.

"I do it like this all the time," she told them.

Problem solved.[2]

That's a great story with a great message for dads. We don't always need words to teach our kids effectively. Sometimes it's best to *give them information* through meaningful actions—with clear consequences attached—and then *let them decide* what to do about it.

The following two-step approach to teaching consequences comes from *Parenting with Love and Logic.*[3]

1. *Offer your children choices.* Control the situation, but transfer the responsibility to your child.

   Examples:

   • If your son is neglecting his lawn-mowing duties, yelling at him probably won't help. Instead, simply tell him, "I'll take you to your soccer game as soon as the lawn is cut." In doing so, you have transferred the responsibility to him. He now has a decision to make—whether to mow the lawn or miss his game. It's his choice. And when you follow through with the consequences of his decision (and he misses the game), you haven't started a fight. You've actually kept a promise and helped him develop his decision-making ability.

   • Tell your daughter she can be polite at the dinner table or she can spend that time in her room and miss a meal.

- Tell her she can clean up her room or she can pay someone else to do it.

2. *Let the consequences do the teaching.* If children end up enduring the consequences, don't rub it in or lecture them on the lesson just learned. Instead, show empathy.

Examples:

- If your son misses a meal as a consequence of a choice he's made and then later complains of hunger, tell him, "I'm sure you are hungry. That's what happens when I miss a meal. Don't worry. We'll be sure to have a good breakfast."
- If his cell phone is cut off because he has gone over on his minutes, tell him that you are sure in case of an emergency, his friends will be able to get in touch with him.

When you empathize and encourage your kids to take responsibility for solving the problem, they won't feel criticized. They'll feel more capable, and they'll take more ownership of their decision to change instead of having it forced upon them. This approach also helps you deal more calmly with problems, mistakes, and other teaching opportunities.

As you teach your children discernment, be sure to display a combination of authority and love.

BALANCE AUTHORITY AND LOVE

When Tony told me his story, he was ashamed about what had happened between his sixteen-year-old daughter and him. Over a short period of time, a string of events had aroused his suspicions about her behavior: a late-night phone call he overheard between his daughter and one of her friends, discovery of some provocative clothing she had purchased, and a new hairstyle. Without consulting anyone else, he assumed that his daughter was sexually involved in a relationship that could ruin her life and disgrace the family. But instead of discussing it with her, Tony summoned her into the "family courtroom" for some interrogation and rigorous cross-examination. Tensions escalated, and the episode ended with Tony slapping his daughter and calling her Jezebel.

Eventually, Tony learned that his suspicions were not accurate; he had jumped to the wrong conclusion. Fortunately, his daughter did not leave home, and though their relationship is hanging on by a thread, they're turning the corner. His daughter was almost certainly looking for someone to validate her beauty, and it never occurred to Tony that he was *da man* she was looking to for encouragement, validation, and respect. She needed his love. Without it, she was struggling. Tony's parenting style, which was authoritarian, harmed his relationship with his daughter. Tony has asked his daughter to forgive him and has pledged to do what it will take to repair their relationship. He is also learning how to balance his authority with love.

In his recent study, "Hardwired to Connect,"[4] David Blankenhorn describes how "authoritative communities" provide the support children need to develop their full potential. Keep in mind that the three common parenting styles are: *authoritative parenting, authoritarian parenting,* and *permissive parenting. Authoritative* parents balance control with support. Overly controlling fathers who provide little support are *authoritarian.* Dads who are all support with no control are considered *permissive.* Authoritative fathers, whom most agree are the most effective fathers, provide a balanced mix of support and authority that enhances the growth of discernment.

According to this study, if you want to be an authoritative father, you will:

- *Be warm and nurturing.* Model good behavior and look for positives in your children. Seek to establish close relationships and mutual goals with them. (In contrast, an authoritarian father primarily focuses on command and control and tends to take a negative tone.)

- *Establish clear limits and expectations.* Be decisive when it comes to setting and maintaining clear standards. (Permissive fathers are usually strong in relationship development but weak in this area. When children are left to define their own boundaries, the results are often tragic.)

- *Have a long-term focus instead of a quick-fix mentality.* This quality helps you adapt to your children's ever-changing needs. While a young child can be easily directed, teens need flexibility for their growing desire and need for independence. (A permissive father might give in to avoid upsetting his young child, not realizing that he is missing an opportunity to teach a hard lesson that the child will benefit from later.)

- *Reflect and transmit what it means to be a good person.* All three styles of fathering can effectively teach respect, ethical behavior, compassion, and other important virtues—though an authoritative approach will present a more balanced example for children to emulate.

- *Encourage spiritual and religious development.* Seek to foster your children's spiritual growth and create opportunities for them to express their faith. Also commit to your own spiritual growth. (Authoritarian fathers might take a "my way or the highway" approach, while permissive fathering would be more apt to let a child "figure it out on his own.")

Dad, what's your fathering style? In what areas are you too authoritarian or too permissive? I urge you to get feedback from others. That can be a valuable step toward becoming a balanced, authoritative father.

DEDICATE THEM TO GOD

This well-known proverb offers a profound insight into how we teach our children to be discerning: "Train up your children in the way they should go, and when they are old, they will not turn from it" (Proverbs 22:6, slightly modified).

Biblical scholars have shown that in the original language, the word used for *train* is used other places in the context of a celebration, such as at the dedication of the temple or another sacred structure. In addition, there is evidence that the word *child* refers to a status rather than a chronological age. It could be translated as "infant," "young man," or a "cadet" who is preparing for military service. The phrase *in the way they should go* means "in the right way." It refers to character and perseverance rather than a particular vocation or desire. So this verse isn't so much about adapting our teaching to the individuality or bent of our children. Rather, it's talking about *dedicating* them to the Lord. When we dedicate our children to God and cultivate their character, our children will learn to outthink the world.

Many parents dedicate their children to God when they are first born, but it's appropriate to dedicate older children as well—to create a special event to publicly give them over to God to be used for His purposes. When we do this, we are giving our children dignity and respect through this celebration, but also added responsibility for their own choices. We give them our blessing, and we commit to continue to be involved in instructing them patiently and correcting them in love. We commit to praying for them, petitioning God to make their paths straight, and praying that they will be able to grasp the depth of His love for them. As time goes by, they can adjust to any new stage of life because we have prepared them, launched them, and given them our blessing every step of the way.

Is that a guarantee that our children will always be discerning and make right choices? Not at all. Some kids will choose rebellion and a destructive lifestyle in spite of our best efforts. We must remember that we live in a fallen world, and sometimes life just isn't fair. But it is a general principle that when we give proper attention to training our children and dedicate them to living a well-ordered life for God, we can confidently expect that they will not totally abandon that training and godly example.

In summary, dads who plant and water the seeds of God's Word in their children's hearts allow their kids to experience consequences, balance authority and love, and dedicate their children to God. These dads are well on their way to teaching their kids to outthink the world through discernment. So Dad, parent your children faithfully, knowing there are no guarantees. Simply give them your best, entrust them to God, and pray that He'll lead them. The rest is up to them.

MEETING THE CHALLENGE

Knowing Your Children

A discerning dad of destiny must be aware of his children and their world. In this fast-paced culture, it can be a real challenge to keep up with our children and be tuned in to their lives.

INSTRUCTIONS:

On a scale of 1 to 5, rank the accuracy of the following statements. Then add your scores and plot your total on the scale below. (You may want to have your child's mother or someone who knows you well take the survey and then compare their answers to yours. If your child no longer lives at home, score yourself as you remember your involvement.)

5 = Mostly True
4 = Somewhat True
3 = Undecided
2 = Somewhat False
1 = Mostly False

1. I have a good handle on how my children's needs change as they grow up. ☐

2. I know what encourages my children the most. ☐

3. I am familiar with my children's friends. ☐

4. I know what motivates my children. ☐

5. I could identify most of my children's recent disappointing experiences. ☐

6. I know how my children's emotional needs change over time. ☐

7. I know my children's gifts and talents. ☐

8. I know the issues my children are dealing with. ☐

TOTAL ☐

PLOT YOUR SCORE:

8	19	27	32	36	40
VERY POOR	POOR	AVERAGE	GOOD	VERY GOOD	

(The scale is not uniform because it is based on norms from a study of 1,516 fathers.)

93

QUESTIONS FOR DISCUSSION AND REFLECTION

As you consider how you scored on this inventory, think about the following questions or discuss them with some other fathers.

1. What are your three best information sources when it comes to staying in touch with your children?

2. In what area(s) of your children's lives do you feel you've "missed it" or want to become more discerning?

3. What one thing did your father need to know about you that would have made him a better father?

4. How can fathers help one another in the area of discernment?

ACTION POINTS

Choose one of the following action points and commit to doing it before you go on to the next chapter (or your next group meeting).

1. Read King Solomon's temple dedication in 1 Kings 8 and his request for discernment in 1 Kings 3:9.

2. Volunteer to coach your child's sports team or help supervise a field trip.

3. Check in regularly with your child's teachers, coaches, and music instructors to gain from their perspective.

4. Write a letter to each of your kids, describing what you've noticed in the last year.

5. Instead of asking yes or no questions, draw your child out with, "What do you think . . . ?" or, "What would you have done . . . ?"

6. Take your teen to lunch and ask what she would like to be doing in ten or fifteen years. Then let the teen ask you.

7. At the dinner table, tell each of your children one quality that you appreciate in them.

8. Visit your child's school today to better understand his world. If possible, have lunch together in the school cafeteria.

9. Praise your child accomplishments and listen to how she reacts.

10. The next time your child's friends visit your house, spend time getting to know them.

CHAPTER 6

PROACTIVELY PASS ON YOUR FAITH

These commandments that I give you today are
to be upon your hearts. Impress them on your
children. Talk about them when you sit at home
and when you walk along the road, when you lie
down and when you get up.

DEUTERONOMY 6:6–7 NIV

Fathers deeply influence their children's ideas about God. What a risk God takes with us! We could easily choose to be poor models of God the Father, and our children might then reject both their heavenly Father and us. But God gave us the Scriptures as a guide, and He trusts us to represent Him well, especially to our kids.

Dad, when you stoop down to tie your son's shoe, you communicate something to him about God. When you buy your daughter clothes for school, you're telling her more about Him. When you read your Bible, you communicate how important your relationship with God is to you. And if your children only see you with your Bible on the way to church, that also communicates something powerful. If you seldom extend forgiveness and mercy to your kids, then it will be easier for them to see God as unforgiving. But if you're able to ask for their forgiveness when you've wronged them, you'll be demonstrating what strong, godly manhood is all about.

Most dads want to be good models. We want our children to aspire to be like us in many ways, including our spiritual commitment. It's a natural desire, but it often leads us to put on false fronts of strength or even perfection. If you want to become a dad of destiny who helps his kids learn to outthink the world, you'll want to be transparent about your own walk with God, meet their spiritual needs, and give them spiritual instruction. Let's take a closer look at each of these goals.

BE TRANSPARENT

In chapter 5 we talked about the importance of courageous vulnerability, of allowing our kids to sometimes see our mistakes, as well as our successes. Such transparency is particularly important when it comes to caring for our children's spiritual lives. Your kids need to see, through your words and deeds, that everyone—including you!—needs God and that without Him, we're all lost.

Our inadequacy can make us adequate when it comes to spiritually equipping our children, because it can make us more aware of our dependence on God. Our children may seem young and innocent now, but someday they'll have to face life's questions and adversities without our help. Our transparency allows them to watch us struggle to live a holy life, succeeding in some ways, failing in others, but always calling out to God for His protection and guidance, His mercy and grace.

So talk with your kids about the times in your life when you faced a challenge that called for trust in God. For what did you trust God? How did He respond? Your kids need to hear about those times when you received mercy in the midst of failure and about the times when God gave you comfort. When you tell your children about how God has worked in your life, they'll see that the same divine care and protection is available to them. You may be a great dad to your children, but you're no match for their heavenly Father.

This type of transparency is even more important when your children enter adolescence. Several years ago, Pauline Sawyers finished her PhD at the University of New Mexico. Her study focused on fathers and adolescents and the transmission of religious values and found that a father's modeling of religious commitment tends to have the most impact on his child's religious beliefs during the preteen years. Dad still has an influence on his children when they are between thirteen and fifteen, but other factors begin to assume more influence, such as the dad's fathering style, the degree of harmony in his marriage, and parent-teen communication habits. By the time children are sixteen, variables such as religious education and relationships with religious authorities have greater impact on their religious beliefs than do parents.[1]

This pattern applies to the transmission of *all* values. As your children mature, they will examine their values and beliefs in a new way, looking beyond you for input. As dads we can choose to accept this and adjust our approach or we can drift to the sidelines. Experience says there's much to be gained from joining in with our kids. Though our influence may not be as strong, we can still have an impact on our teenagers.

As your teen enters adolescence—while you may be negotiating the trickiness of midlife—both of you may be doing some deep searching and asking some important identity questions. According to youth-culture specialist Walt Mueller, teenagers are answering these three questions:

1. Who am I—or, what makes me different from everyone else?

2. Who are my friends—or, where do I fit in?

3. Where am I going—or, what does my future look like?[2]

In *The Seasons of a Man's Life,* Daniel Levinson says that during midlife, men are asking these questions, which are strikingly similar to the questions asked in adolescence:

1. What have I done with my life?

2. What do I really get from and give to my wife, children, friends, work, community, and myself?

3. What is it I truly want for myself and others?[3]

Wise is the dad who takes advantage of these similarities and uses them as points of connection with his teens. Many fathers withdraw when their children become teenagers, but this can actually be a time of mutual learning and sharing. Since you may be going through a similar kind of soul searching, you can probably empathize and offer a helpful perspective if you are willing to be transparent. This time of mutual searching can become a point of connection that can positively impact your teenager's faith.

Adolescence does not have to be a period when you simply "survive" as a dad. Be open. Don't pretend that you have instant answers. Walk beside your child on his journey, even if the terrain seems rough. Keep in mind that support and care create a more positive environment for communication with your teen, but harshness and authoritarianism typically result in rejection and alienation between a father and his teen.

Children who encounter Christian ideals and God's Word only a couple of hours a week at church will likely grow up to believe that their faith need not permeate the rest of their life. Such children may talk the talk on Sunday mornings, but during the week they may be weak and yield to the majority. Dads who are transparent will counteract this tendency.

But it's not enough to simply be transparent. If you want your kids to develop a strong faith of their own, you must also be involved in the care of their spiritual lives.

MEET THEIR SPIRITUAL NEEDS

In her book *They Still Pick Me Up When I Fall*, Diana Rauner presents an insightful model that challenges us to become caring people and build caring communities. I believe that dads who want to cultivate the spiritual lives of their children can benefit from applying her three "caring" components to ensure they meet the spiritual needs of their children.[4]

1. *Attentiveness.* Pay attention to your children. Observe them and gather information that helps you understand their spiritual needs. If you don't, your attempts to develop the spiritual life of your children may become mechanical or formulistic. A lack of attentiveness conveys a lack of respect, as though your children are not worth investing the time to know them as unique individuals.

   The best way to be attentive to your kids is through an activity, communication, and listening. One dad I know takes one of his children out to breakfast every Saturday morning.

   His kids look forward to the pancakes or bagels, but they also enjoy the one-on-one time they get with Dad. For a small price and an hour of time, this father gets one of his children all to himself. He doesn't use the time to impart some spiritual lesson; rather, he listens. He simply hangs out with the child. As he builds a close relationship with each of his kids, this dad is increasing the likelihood that he will be aware of the spiritual needs of his children. He's also building trust so that his kids will listen to him later, when a teachable moment comes along.

Other examples of attentiveness include:

- Asking them to explain or describe what they think or feel about God, then listening to what they say.

- Asking them to describe how they see God working in their lives.

- Talking after church or a family devotional about what they received from the experience.

2. *Responsiveness.* If you see a need, spring into action. Being responsive to your children will be a gateway to their further revelation of God. The book of Luke concludes with a good example of how Jesus was responsive to people's spiritual needs. After His death and resurrection, two men were returning home to Emmaus and discussing all that had recently transpired in the capital city that week, namely the crucifixion and mysterious disappearance of the body of Jesus. An apparent stranger—Jesus—joins them and their discussion, helping them make sense of the prophetic words in the Old Testament, as well as matching them to the events they were discussing. Jesus revealed himself to these men, and "he opened their minds so they could understand

the Scriptures" (Luke 24:45 NIV). Like Jesus, we can respond to opportunities to nurture our children's faith.

It's often the little things that make a big difference, and one of the best ways to be responsive is through prayer. For example, at bedtime, ask your children about their individual concerns and then pray with them for those needs. You'll find yourself praying for animals, world events, friends at school, and people with illnesses.

3. *Competence.* Competence as a dad is neither a state of mind nor a way of thought; it's knowing what to say to your kids and how to say it, what to do and how to do it. It is knowing when (and being able) to refrain from action, even when your strongest impulses are to act.

   Brothers, here's where we need to shine. Make certain your kids receive the best by wisely evaluating the churches, youth groups, and schools your children attend. Keep your promises, follow through on your commitments, and demonstrate a caring attitude.

   Though we will never be perfectly competent in our fathering, our Father is. When we seek to grow in our faith, we unite the resources of earth with the power of heaven so that we give our kids the best of fathering from two worlds. But if we fail to live a dynamic life of faith, we will also pass on this same attitude to our children.

Each of these qualities works together. Attentiveness prepares the ground for responsiveness, and responsiveness requires competence; they work together and depend on each other. While caring for our children spiritually, we consider the impact of our actions while doing the caring action.

Many of us will have to learn and practice these caring skills, and it's worth our efforts to improve. They can transform our lives and our relationships with our children. While our care for their spiritual development does not guarantee our children a place in heaven, it does help to increase their awareness of God's love and their opportunities to witness the powerful difference He makes in people's lives.

So will our instruction in God's Word.

TEACH THEM GOD'S WORD

In this information-based society, we have an immense database of facts, figures, and deep thoughts at our disposal. Still, our greatest resource is the most underused. God's Word is essential for us to have the mind of Christ and live a fulfilling and rich life. Dad, don't make the mistake of focusing on all the information this world has produced but neglecting biblical insight. More than anything else, God's Word equips us to outthink the world.

When I'm teaching fifteen boys in a fourth-grade Sunday school class at our church, I often ask so-called Bible trivia questions, such as, what's the fifth commandment? Or, who was Moses's father-in-law? These may seem simple, but your children need this kind of knowledge if they are going to outthink the world. When kids know those stories and the truths behind them, they can apply biblical truth to

In the 1600s William Gouge argued for making sure that we did not institutionalize our children's spiritual training to the Church, as he reminded householders that each home was "a little church and a little commonwealth, at least a lively representation thereof, whereby trial may be made for such as are fit for any place of authority or subjection to the church or commonwealth."[5]

real-life situations and even communicate it to others. When they have internalized God's Word, they will have the mind of Christ, as Paul described in 1 Corinthians 2:16: "For *who has* understood *the mind of the Lord* so as to *instruct him?* But we have the mind of Christ" (emphasis added).

Here is an example: My oldest daughter, Hannah, has the gift of evangelism, and she used that gift effectively during her years at the university. God led her to join and live in a sorority and share the love of Christ with her sorority sisters. One night, when a group of girls had gathered for a chapter meeting, someone put on a video showing explicit and disgusting adult material—and many of the girls were making equally shocking comments. Hannah got up and left the room, and two younger girls followed her. They asked Hannah what was going on, and she told them why she was outraged. Then she added, "That video that someone slipped in at the chapter meeting is like Sodom and Gomorrah, and we have to cut that kind of stuff out of our house's tradition."

One of the girls looked puzzled. "Hannah, what's Sodom and Gomorrah?" She didn't know the biblical story and the meaning it carries as a reference to unrestrained sexual behavior. So, right then and there, Hannah gave a little sorority-house Sunday school lesson. When she was finished, one girl asked, "You mean God wiped out cities because they were involved in that type of activity?"

Hannah took the opportunity to talk about why it is critical to stay pure and holy, even during the collegiate years. She then challenged her sisters to take a hard look at whether their own choices were pleasing to God. Over time, God used that experience and others like it to communicate truth to those young women, and for at least one of them, it led to a relationship with Jesus Christ and a transformed life. That's the kind of thing that can happen when children are prepared to outthink this world by applying God's truth.

Dad, put Deuteronomy 6:4–7 into practice in your home:

Hear, O Israel: The Lord our God, the Lord is one. Love the Lord your God with all your heart and with all your soul and with all your strength. These commandments that I give you today are to be upon your hearts. Impress them on your children. Talk about them when you sit at home and when you walk along the road, when you lie down and when you get up. (NIV)

God wants our households to be a primary place of spiritual training, especially when it comes to matters of faith. The temple, the synagogue, and the church have secondary responsibility, so train, explain, educate, and teach God's truths to your kids.

Yes, mothers also have a responsibility to train their children in spiritual matters, and they have often stepped in where fathers have been negligent. But God has placed the primary responsibility upon fathers as loving, serving leaders and teachers in their households.

I know this isn't easy. Maybe your wife has settled into this role, and that seems to work fine. Or it may be that just being in the same room with your children challenges you. Maybe the thought of trying to talk about anything significant seems a joke. I understand. But be warned: God wants fathers to teach their families to live by His revelations, and dads who disregard that role may suffer some serious consequences.

To teach your kids God's Word you can:

1. *Fix or establish the Word of God in your own mind.* Before you can teach your kids about God's Word and His commandments, you need to know it yourself. Study it until

His commandments fill your thoughts. His Word should be very familiar to you, and you should be in the regular habit of applying it to your life. Not only will this prepare you to teach your children, it will also set an example for them of what a life of faith looks like.

But don't wait until you know God's Word better to begin talking about it with your kids. Start today by talking about what you do know—and keep in mind that you don't have to rely on your own abilities but on the God who called you to this role (who will also equip you for this role).

2. *Be intentional about teaching God's Word.* It takes effort and planning to teach biblical truths to our kids. Bring all your planning and creative resources into the picture.

- Use books, devotional guides, videos, and CDs to add an age-appropriate spark to your efforts to teach God's Word.

- Memorize Scripture together. As your children grow and mature, help them learn simple, familiar verses: the Lord's model prayer from Matthew 6, the Twenty-third Psalm, John 3:16, the beatitudes from Matthew 5, and your own favorites. Put these verses on an index card and post them on the fridge or family bulletin board and memorize them along with your kids. Repeat them to each other in the morning, at bedtime, or at the dinner table.

- If you know your child is dealing with a specific issue— at school, on a sports team, or relating to his friends—

look up a specific verse that speaks to that issue and say, "Hey, let's memorize this together." It can bring you closer together and be a daily reminder that you care about what your children are dealing with every day. Even better, your actions will remind them God cares about their situation.

- As your children become more independent and eventually leave your home, you can continue to use God's Word as a steady connection point. When you talk with them on the phone, remind them of the verses you memorized together as a family. Include them on cards and at the end of letters. The Bible can be common ground in your relationship for your entire life.

3. *Include discussion and illustration in your teaching.* Moses urges us to "talk about" God's precepts; he doesn't tell us to lecture or use Scripture to try to win an argument. So look for ways to engage your children spiritually:

- Ask about their opinions concerning biblical truths.

- Bounce ideas off them.

- If your kids are older, engage them in deep discussions about faith by asking questions about spiritual matters: What are you most thankful for this week? Who's someone in your class that we can be praying for? Or, what's the one difficulty for which you'd like some support?

4. *Teach continuously and consistently.* Scripture says to teach biblical precepts when you sit at home, walk along the road, when you lie down, when you get up (see

Deuteronomy 6:7). So help your children understand and apply God's Word during the day-to-day routine of life: in the car, on the playing field, at the supermarket, around the dinner table, or in the garage. For example:

- Extend grace to your children. They won't always choose the path you hoped they would. Give thanks anyway. They'll mess up; they'll get into trouble. Thank God for them and don't close yourself off from them. Make thanksgiving an attitude that you carry throughout your life as a father—no matter what. Job said, "Shall we accept good from God, and not trouble?" (Job 2:10 NIV). And the writer of Hebrews urges us, "Since we are receiving a kingdom that cannot be shaken, let us be thankful" (12:28 NIV). Your gratitude will demonstrate to your children what real faith is all about.

- Take advantage of teachable moments that lend themselves to discussions about integrity, honesty, and purity.

- Use the experiences of daily life to talk with them about what God's Word has to say about overcoming temptation, delaying gratification, handling anger or jealousy or greed.

- Help them understand that we glorify God when we do our best and remain faithful to Him during hard times.[6]

One of the most important things you can do, however, when it comes to having a positive influence on your children's faith, is to spend time with them. Take up the motto of a dad I know: "Always take a kid along." When this father heads to the hardware store, the auto mechanic, the grocery store, he always takes one of his kids. Away from the rest of the family, he and the child have a little more of each other's attention. This effective father uses everyday errands wisely, knowing that the soil of *quantity* time is where *quality* time is most likely to spring up. Again, his focus is the relationship. If something happens and he gets to model honesty or service to someone else, that's a bonus.

A QUESTION OF *HOW,* NOT *IF*

Your children are spiritual beings. They can no more decide whether to have a spirit than they can decide whether to be human. So the question is not *if* they will develop spiritually, but rather *how well* or *how poorly* their spiritual life will be developed. A large part of that, Dad, is up to you.

Our kids can become a generation of creative, truth-filled thinkers who can help to solve some of the big social and medical problems of our day, such as teen pregnancy or the AIDS virus. We need to give them the spiritual instruction they need to be in sync with God's inspired and inspiring revelation so they can meet the challenges ahead and win the world for Christ. If your kids live in God's Word, they may develop insights that could change the world. No matter what their IQs are, as God's children they will have access to wisdom and power that can equip them to outthink this fallen world.

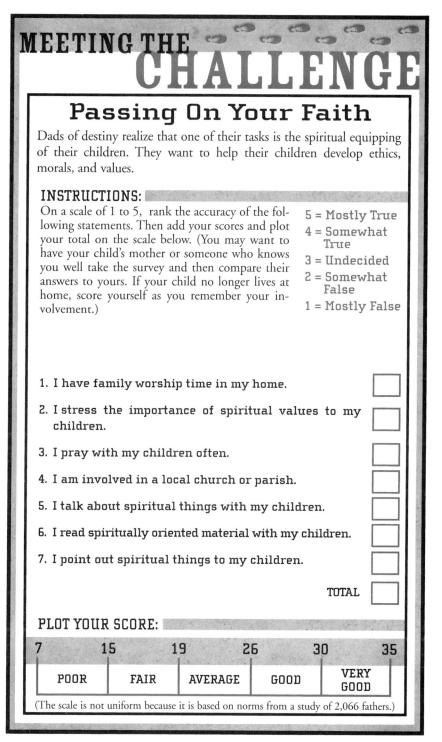

MEETING THE CHALLENGE

Passing On Your Faith

Dads of destiny realize that one of their tasks is the spiritual equipping of their children. They want to help their children develop ethics, morals, and values.

INSTRUCTIONS:

On a scale of 1 to 5, rank the accuracy of the following statements. Then add your scores and plot your total on the scale below. (You may want to have your child's mother or someone who knows you well take the survey and then compare their answers to yours. If your child no longer lives at home, score yourself as you remember your involvement.)

5 = Mostly True
4 = Somewhat True
3 = Undecided
2 = Somewhat False
1 = Mostly False

1. I have family worship time in my home. ☐

2. I stress the importance of spiritual values to my children. ☐

3. I pray with my children often. ☐

4. I am involved in a local church or parish. ☐

5. I talk about spiritual things with my children. ☐

6. I read spiritually oriented material with my children. ☐

7. I point out spiritual things to my children. ☐

TOTAL ☐

PLOT YOUR SCORE:

7	15	19	26	30	35
POOR	FAIR	AVERAGE	GOOD	VERY GOOD	

(The scale is not uniform because it is based on norms from a study of 2,066 fathers.)

QUESTIONS FOR DISCUSSION AND REFLECTION

As you consider how you scored on this inventory, think about the following questions or discuss them with some other fathers.

1. How has your relationship with your father influenced your perceptions of God?

2. What is the biggest difficulty you have in guiding your children spiritually?

3. What role does worship play in the task of spiritually equipping your children?

4. What specifically do you want to teach your children about spiritual growth?

5. Who are the other significant spiritual role models for your children?

ACTION POINTS

Choose one of the following action points and commit to doing it before you go on to the next chapter (or your next group meeting).

1. Search the Scriptures with your children for verses that apply to struggles they are going through.

2. At the next family crisis, gather the whole family together for prayer to demonstrate your dependence on God.

3. Write a meaningful paragraph in your child's Bible and then sign it, "Your earthly father."

4. After church on Sunday, ask your kids, "What part of the service did you enjoy most?"

5. Read the parable of the Good Samaritan with your children, then ask them who at school needs their friendship and mercy.

6. As a family, abstain from something you enjoy (food, entertainment, activities) for an agreed upon period of time to consider spiritual matters.

7. Share your spiritual pilgrimage with your children; tell them a high point and low point of the adventure.

8. Before you leave for work, touch each of your children and "God bless" them in regard to their day.

9. Write each of your children a letter and include a spiritual blessing appropriate to them.

10. Ask your children to lead the family in a devotional time.

CHAPTER 7

BE THEIR PRIMARY EDUCATOR

In days to come, when your son asks you,
"What does this mean?" say [this] to him . . .

EXODUS 13:14 NIV

Clark is a dedicated husband and father who wrote an article for the National Center for Fathering several years ago. In the article he talked about a letter he'd received from his son's school just before the fall semester. The letter contained information about the schedule and parking and then went on to explain what was expected from all parties in the educational process: the student, the teachers and administrators, and the parents. The letter suggested that the parents' role was to see that their children got proper nourishment and rest. That was it.

Now, to be fair to that school, its teachers and administrators had probably learned from experience that some parents don't want to be involved much more than that. But as a dedicated father who took his son's education very seriously, Clark was offended. He wrote a response letter, saying that *he* was the ultimate educator of his child, and he appreciated the opportunity to *use the school* to help in that process. He went on to say that he would be monitoring his son's learning experiences in the classroom to make sure they were consistent with his family's knowledge, faith, and goals.

Like Clark, more and more fathers are recognizing what others have been advocating for a long time: parents need to be *more involved* in their children's education. Some writers have been quite adamant about this. William Barclay observed this about the benefit of parental involvement in shaping the spiritual values of the home: "The New Testament knows nothing about religious education and nothing about schools, for the New Testament is certain that the only training which really matters is given within the home, and that there are no teachers so effective for good or evil as parents are."[1] Richard Baxter, a famous Puritan preacher, pointed out that parents are the most effective educators of their children because "(1) there are fewer to teach; (2) the students are always with you and you may speak often and (3) they are tied to you by relation, affection and covenant."[2]

God ordained that we should be our children's primary educators. Paul wasn't writing to church leaders or teachers when he stressed the importance of bringing up children "in the training and instruction of the Lord" (Ephesians 6:4 NIV). He was talking to us as fathers. He was talking to you.

Like Clark, you can reclaim this responsibility and privilege. If you want your kids to outthink the world, get involved in their education.

DON'T LEAVE THE JOB TO THE SCHOOL

Your children will spend the majority of their growing-up years in a classroom, getting an education. Gifted teachers and other school district resources can be great blessings, but make sure you are informed enough and involved enough to look out for your children's best interests. Make appropriate decisions regarding their education and be an advocate for them when necessary.

Don't assume that their public school will give your kids everything they need, particularly when it comes to having "the mind of Christ." For one thing, much of today's school curriculum doesn't take biblical truth into account. Many teachers tell their students that truth can't be taught or revealed. Instead, they claim that truth is relative and that individuals can come to their own understanding of truth.

If you see yourself as their primary educator, you will increase your influence on your kids' lives when they need it most: when they are sorting through various philosophies and world-views. If you stay connected with them and monitor their educational development, you will be able to guide and encourage your kids toward things that are true, noble, right, pure, lovely, admirable, excellent and praiseworthy (see Philippians 4:8 NIV).

In my work with adolescent daughters, I ask them to complete this statement: I wish I could talk to my dad about _____. One of the most common responses is that they wish for more guidance from their fathers: "Where will I go to college?" "What will my future be?" "Whom will I marry?" "What do I want to be?"[3]

More and more fathers are doing this. Many place a high priority on schoolwork and are involved in helping their kids schedule time each day for homework in order to ensure that they follow through with assignments. Some dads take it a step further: we sharpen a pencil, sit at the dining room table, and act like we really do remember all those algebra equations.

Some families are so passionate about their children's education that they homeschool them. These moms and dads want their kids to benefit from the potential advantages of homeschooling: flexibility, a personalized approach, and control over the curriculum. If you and your wife want to do this and can make the schedule work, this is a great option. But it isn't the only option. You can still be involved in your children's education. Let's look at some practical ideas for how to do this.

BE INVOLVED AT YOUR CHILD'S SCHOOL

Consider participating in your child's education in some of the following ways:

- Have lunch with your child at school.

- Offer to help with school productions, carnivals, field trips, or parent-child activities.

- Attend parent association meetings to stay current on what's happening at your child's school.

- Apply for a position on the school board if you have the time and interest to fill that role.

- Be a sponsor or assistant for a sports team or club.

- Tutor kids who need help.

- Volunteer one day a year at your child's school, as do many dads who participate in our WatchDOGS (Dads of Great Students) programs.[4]

- Pray in specific ways for your children's teachers and administrators, as well as for their friends and classmates. Pray for your children's performance, as well as for their being a light for Christ.

When you are active at your children's school, you have a natural way to connect with them on their turf. You can also be a positive influence for other children who need an adult who cares—not to mention teachers, who can always use some assistance.

Reading together offers you a second way to get more involved in your children's education.

READ OFTEN WITH YOUR CHILDREN

Why the emphasis on reading? Why not math or science or some other subject? Because how well a person reads impacts his or her ability and desire to read God's Word. Consider the following:

- In 1644 Massachusetts enacted a law that stated that heads of households should be responsible for teaching their children to read.[5]

- In 1647 the General Court of Massachusetts provided for the establishment of reading schools for the colony because it was "one chief project of that old deluder, Satan, to keep men from the knowledge of the Scriptures."[6]

- It soon became standard practice throughout early America to enhance opportunities to read, not simply as an accomplishment or a way to financially improve one's status, but "because salvation was impossible without it." In those days, there was a general sense that one of man's chief enemies was ignorance, specifically "ignorance of the Scriptures."[7]

Dad, if you want your kids to outthink the world, be sure they have the necessary skill to read and understand God's Word. That's what Robert did, and his commitment had significant dividends.

Robert's son Daniel was struggling with his second-grade reading lessons, and none of the school's extra measures to help Daniel seemed to bring much improvement. So Robert decided to get more directly involved. Each morning before school, he and Daniel got up early and sat together on the living-room couch, taking turns reading verses aloud from the book of Proverbs. They sometimes came across words that stretched Daniel's abilities or principles that Daniel didn't understand. When this happened Robert did his best to patiently explain the meaning, knowing that Daniel would benefit from both the process of reading and the wisdom they talked about during those morning sessions.

After about three months, Daniel's teacher sent home a note saying that Daniel had shown remarkable progress. Over the next three or four years, Daniel made more positive strides and now he consistently scores near the top of his class in English and reading comprehension.

As Robert discovered:

- *Reading brings you into close proximity with your young child.* People can watch television from opposite sides of the room. Not so when reading together. You sit side by side, sharing the same book, looking at the pictures together.

- *Reading aloud forces you to be interesting.* It's nearly impossible to read a children's book without changing your voice for different characters, acting scared or surprised, and involving yourself in the story line. As you exhibit different emotions with your children, you are helping them understand how to express their feelings to you.

- *Reading with your children gives you a chance to observe and enjoy them.* I used to love watching my son Micah react to a story I was reading. He'd think, wonder, worry, and smile. Your children's responses will give you clues about who they are and what they need most from you.

- *Reading together allows you to teach your values and monitor your child's level of understanding and mental maturity.* During the story you can ask questions like, "What does that mean?" "Why do you think he did that?" or, "What do you think you would have done?" C. S. Lewis books are great for this. When you ask questions such as these, you can learn more about what your kids are thinking.

   Reading together also allows you to teach character qualities. For example, if you're seeking to teach a young man about courage, read a story that displays it powerfully, and then ask him to role-play a portion of the story in which the character displays courage. Or ask him to draw a picture of what courage looks like to him.

- *The rewards of reading together—for both of you—are immeasurable.* You will learn together, grow together. Your kids may even begin to teach you. When my oldest child, Hannah, began reading "real" books, the world opened up to her. She began learning things that I couldn't teach her. And sometimes she'd even recommend a book to me. That was a thrill that I didn't anticipate as a father—that my kids could help teach me. But the biggest thrill was catching them—on their own—reading from God's Word.

So, Dads, read to and with your children. As often as you can. Share a newspaper; hit the library or bookstore together. Read aloud to them or have them read aloud to you. Have a family quiet time in which everyone has his or her own book.

Reading is powerful. It leads to laughter, tears, deep questions, and great discussions—it's a great way of bonding with your child.

Much of what's important in life isn't taught at school: lessons about morals, family relationships, faith, how to care for ourselves and our possessions—the list goes on and on. Dad, if you want to teach your kids how to outthink the world, your involvement in their education needs to extend much further than their formal learning.

EXPAND YOUR DEFINITION OF EDUCATION

View the process of educating your children as a *way of life* and an ongoing opportunity to pass on a legacy of who you are and what you believe. Always be looking for opportunities to teach a life skill, talk about a value-driven decision, or model a way of life. Think of outings that will expand your children's horizons or challenge their thinking. Encourage them to take on challenges that will help develop their character.

In addition:

1. *Find ways to engage your kids.* Instead of lecturing them, tell them stories. Use word pictures that appeal to them. Plan "field trips" to expose them to new experiences. Get their minds churning, and the lessons you teach will be long remembered.

2. *Keep it short and simple.* If you launch into a five-minute lecture or jump on a soapbox, your kids will tune you out and miss the point. Just point out a life truth that is readily apparent, and trust that your child will grasp it for future use.

3. *Study your children.* Good teachers know what appeals to their individual students. Likewise, you can identify your kids' learning styles so that you can teach them more ef-

fectively. For example, most kids fit in one of three categories of learners: (1) talkers and listeners, (2) doers and touchers, (3) watchers.

If you know your child is a "doer and toucher," you'll avoid putting him in situations that require sitting still for long periods of time. If you know your child is an auditory learner (talker and listener), you'll be more likely to explain things rather than direct her to read the instructions— you'll encourage her to listen to tapes rather than read books.

Also study your children so you know their temperament. Your daughter may keep trying and trying until she learns to ride that bicycle, but your son may give up after one crash and not try again until a few years have passed. Some kids like structure, some thrive with background music and indirect light, some do their best early in the morning, and some need to bounce ideas off others.

You don't need to become an expert at these things, but the more sensitive you are to your children's learning styles and preferences, the better you can help them learn. (For more information about learning styles and temperament, read *Unlocking Your Child's Learning Potential* by Cheri Fuller.)

4. *Don't always give your children final answers to their questions.* Answer with questions that encourage them to think, and help brainstorm ways to find the answers.

5. *Share some of your own challenges with your children.* Invite them into the process of solving a problem so they

can watch you deal with the setback and come up with a plan for resolving it. Be sure to thank them for whatever suggestions or ideas they offer—no matter how outlandish.

CREATE A POSITIVE VISION FOR THEIR FUTURE

Your kids need a dad who is thinking about and preparing them for their future, whether that's tomorrow, next week, next year, or ten years from now. While our kids' development is ultimately up to them, we can play an important supporting and encouraging role. So:

1. *Cast a positive vision for their future.* Do you cast a vision for each of your children? To see how you're doing in this area, consider your words. If your words express doubt or uncertainty about your children's futures, you can devastate them.

   For example: If you tell your daughter, "Don't worry about doing well in geometry; it might be over your head," she'll believe it and will grow up associating math with frustration. If you tell her, "Go easy on the sweets, Honey. You know boys don't date overweight girls," she may just prove you right. Or she may become obsessed with proving you wrong and take dangerous measures to be thin, or she may throw herself at the first boy who shows her some positive attention.

   Your children's ability to achieve their potential depends in part on your resolve to appreciate them and cast a positive vision for their future. Here are some ideas for how to do that:

- Be sensitive to their gifts and aspirations. Ask, "What are your dreams?" then be ready to listen and encourage.

- Make positive, specific comments but also leave room for your children to make their own choices. For example: "God has given you such a sensitive heart. I wouldn't be surprised if you end up helping a lot of people in your lifetime." Even if their goals seem somewhat outlandish, be optimistic. Tell each of your kids that God has great things in store for them.

- Make sure they know they don't have to earn your approval. Tell them you love them—no matter what—and say it over and over. Repetition has the power to change behavior, and you can use it to affirm your children and give them a vision for what's ahead.

2. *Have a plan.* You've heard the saying: if you fail to plan, you have planned to fail. Dad, let's come up with a plan right now to equip our children to succeed. Several different areas come to mind:

- Talk with them about their vocational future. Help them see how they can develop and express their talents in ways that please God.

- Help them plan for their relational future. Start talking *now* about what to look for in a mate. Pray together for that little girl or young man. Also, discuss what it takes to make a marriage work, and the idea that *finding* the right person is really more about *becoming* the right person.

- Provide some rites of passage—benchmarks along the way that help signal new levels of maturity and responsibility, and that affirm them and bless them as beloved children.

- Make a list of the skills, attitudes, and values you want to instill in your kids by the time they leave home. Go ahead and write them down. Include financial stewardship, the ability to delay gratification, prayer, basic auto maintenance, thankfulness, perseverance, honesty, the value of hard work, modesty, or family togetherness. Check that list from time to time as a reminder.

BE AN EXPERT ENCOURAGER

As your kid's primary educator, know that they will inevitably fail at times. Failure is part of learning and development. As a matter of fact, if your kids don't fail once in a while, they are not being challenged enough. But you can help them turn each setback into a learning experience.

Dad, your unwavering confidence in your children can lift them to new goals and achievements. It will help them recognize and count on your support and strengthen your relationship with them. What's more, your encouragement may inspire in your children a desire—or even a love—for learning. That's perhaps one of the highest goals in the task of educating your children.

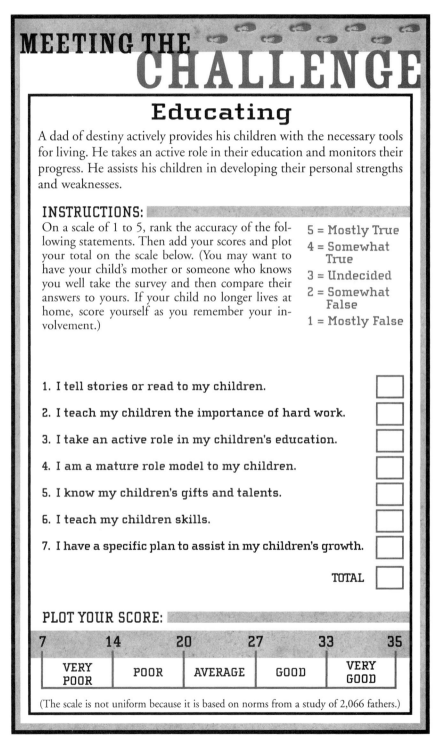

MEETING THE CHALLENGE

Educating

A dad of destiny actively provides his children with the necessary tools for living. He takes an active role in their education and monitors their progress. He assists his children in developing their personal strengths and weaknesses.

INSTRUCTIONS:

On a scale of 1 to 5, rank the accuracy of the following statements. Then add your scores and plot your total on the scale below. (You may want to have your child's mother or someone who knows you well take the survey and then compare their answers to yours. If your child no longer lives at home, score yourself as you remember your involvement.)

5 = Mostly True
4 = Somewhat True
3 = Undecided
2 = Somewhat False
1 = Mostly False

1. I tell stories or read to my children. ☐

2. I teach my children the importance of hard work. ☐

3. I take an active role in my children's education. ☐

4. I am a mature role model to my children. ☐

5. I know my children's gifts and talents. ☐

6. I teach my children skills. ☐

7. I have a specific plan to assist in my children's growth. ☐

TOTAL ☐

PLOT YOUR SCORE:

7	14	20	27	33	35
VERY POOR	POOR	AVERAGE	GOOD	VERY GOOD	

(The scale is not uniform because it is based on norms from a study of 2,066 fathers.)

QUESTIONS FOR DISCUSSION AND REFLECTION

As you consider how you scored on this inventory, think about the following questions or discuss them with some other fathers.

1. What are the most important lessons you want your children to learn about life?

2. What kind of learner is your child?

3. How can you encourage your children to excel in their education?

4. What are three specific things you could do to be more involved in your children's education?

5. Who influences you the most as you think about being involved in your children's education? What does he or she do that impresses you?

ACTION POINTS

Choose one of the following action points and commit to doing it before you go on to the next chapter (or your next group meeting).

1. Expose your children to other cultures by inviting ethnic and international friends to your home.

2. Ask your children what is the one thing you do that they would like to learn, and then teach it.

3. Put an encouraging note in the textbook of your child's least favorite subject.

4. Teach your older children to check and add oil to the car.

5. Take your children to the library and give them thirty minutes to browse and check out some books.

6. Discuss with your children some goals for the school year—theirs and yours.

7. Encourage your children to join various clubs and organizations.

8. Help your high schooler research prospective colleges and send off for catalogs.

9. Listen to your children recite their prayers; teach them a simple one.

10. Ask your children what they want to be when they grow up, and then take them to visit such a workplace.

PART THREE

Outliving the World

Living above the world requires out-of-this-world power and discipline. As sons of another Father, dads of destiny have the presence of the Holy Spirit living in them as an ally in our quest to *outlive* the world. Fathers who walk in cadence with the Spirit can resist the temptation to forsake their fathering role and to compromise their integrity. The children of these fathers, by example, come to understand self-control and discipline. They also grow up securely attached to a household that models a functioning marriage and family. This example becomes the foundation for building a legacy that will equip future generations to outlive the world.

CHAPTER 8

WALK YOUR TALK

The Son [does] . . . what he sees the Father doing.
JOHN 5:19

Modeling is where our true influence as dads of destiny shows up, because godliness is *caught* more than it is *taught*. The challenge to be a positive role model for our kids is one we will face every day of our earthly existence. Our children, like private eyes, are watching our every move. They're taking mental notes. They learn more from watching us than from listening to what we say. Many of our actions will form the building blocks of their character and influence their views about life and faith. Each day, in hundreds of ways, we communicate to our kids, "Follow me."

This presents both a dilemma and an opportunity. It's a dilemma because our children *will* use our lives as reference points, for better or worse, by design or by default. It's also an opportunity to be intentional about demonstrating what a responsible, calm, caring, self-sacrificing, faith-filled father is like.

Bruce is a retired pastor, committed to passing on a legacy of faith to his children and grandchildren. Recently, one of our staff told me about an experience that was remarkably simple, yet incredibly powerful. He and his wife were driving somewhere, along with two of their grandchildren, who were in elementary school. The radio was on, and Bruce was barely paying attention to it, but the children heard something on the news that confused them.

The grandson asked, "Grandpa, why would any husband kill his wife?" It's the kind of question you're never expecting and never quite ready to answer. But Bruce handled it admirably. He said, "Well, I don't know. I can't imagine why anyone would do something like that, but I do know that your dad would never kill your mom, and I would certainly never kill your grandmother."

> Example is the school of mankind, and we learn from no other.
>
> EDMUND BURKE

That's when his granddaughter piped up from the backseat. "That's right, Grandpa, because you're a godly man. You read your Bible and pray every morning."

Bruce's jaw dropped, and he had tears in his eyes as he told the story. He never even knew his granddaughter had noticed his morning habit of reading the Bible, much less that she would associate it with godly behavior.

If we want to be a dad of destiny, we will need to balance our internal commitments with our external actions, to practice what we preach. Our children need to see consistency in us. Even Jesus was highly dependent on the example set by His Father. He once said, "The Son . . . can do only what he sees his Father doing, because whatever the Father does the Son also does" (John 5:19 NIV).[1]

"A son does what he sees his father doing." Everything you do is under a microscope. What do your kids catch you doing? What are you teach-

ing them about what's most important in life? How does your modeling affect the way your sons will treat women or the way your daughters will relate to men? How does the way you treat others impact your children's expectations? How does your devotion to God affect your children's perception of their heavenly Father?

Many children who grew up with hypocritical fathers talk about the anger, disbelief, and desperation that are their inheritance. What father would choose to have that kind of impact on his children? And yet that is possible . . . unless we make a concerted effort to have a life-giving impact on our kids. Fathers have extraordinary power in modeling the behavior we desire our children to emulate. If we walk what we talk and lead by example, we will shape the next generation in a lasting way. That's why our words and deeds must be in harmony. They represent the lifeblood of our commitment.

Let's look at four key areas in which dads of destiny model godliness: marriage, relationship with God, emotions, and character.

MODEL LOVE AND COMMITMENT IN MARRIAGE

John became a husband and a father on the same day. He married Debra and became a stepfather to Stacy. He was committed to putting Debra first and showing love to his six-year-old stepdaughter. For mom and daughter, John brought the care and stability they had missed and longed for.

Then about three years later, Stacy approached her stepdad with a simple, but significant, request: "Will you adopt me?"

Her biological father was never in the picture, but the request caught John by surprise. "You want me to adopt you? Why, Stacy?"

"Because I see how much joy you've brought into my mom's life, and I want it too."

That's quite a statement, and it shows that our kids catch what we model. We need to provide them with a healthy model for masculine behavior toward women. We do it because we love our wives, and that's how we keep our marriages healthy. But we also do it to show our sons how to love and serve women and to help our daughters understand what to expect from the men in their lives.

What is your son learning from you about how to be a husband? Russell was thinking of leaving his family. His wife was having serious emotional problems, his teenage daughters were unruly, and his nine-year-old son seemed lost in life. He wasn't even going to tell the girls, but he wanted to have a talk with his son. He took the boy outside on the front porch. As Russell was about to break the news, his son chimed in: "Hey, Dad, do you know what I've learned from you? When the going gets tough, us guys, we stick it out." Russell says it was as if the voice of God had come right out of his nine-year-old son and grabbed him by the heart. He's still in the marriage, and it isn't easy; but he's trying to make things better. Most of all, he's showing his son that working through problems in a marriage is the right thing to do.

What are your actions telling your daughter about what to look for in a husband? Are you training her to spot counterfeits? If you want her to marry a godly man, make sure she is familiar with the real thing. She needs lots of your attention, affirmation, and healthy physical affection. But make it clear to her that she has won your heart because she is a fascinating and worthwhile person. As her father, you can show her how a proper, respectful man behaves—and if you do, she'll be able to see through the irresponsible, insensitive, dishonest men she meets along the way.

If you and your wife model a strong marriage—not faking it, but really doing the work, the communication, the thoughtful gestures—

you will create powerful and lasting pictures for your children. See to it that your kids understand why some people talk about their marriage or their spouse with a sparkle in their eye. That, more than anything else, will convince them that marriage is worth waiting for.

Here are practical ideas for how you can be a positive role model regarding marriage:

- Spend meaningful time with your wife away from the kids. Let them know why you're doing it and that you'll be having a great time together.

- Enlist your children's help in doing something special for your wife, whether it's making a gift, shopping for one, or cleaning the house—including the bathroom.

- When you tuck your kids into bed, pray for their mother and thank God for the blessing she has been to you.

- Tell your kids about how you were inspired by the lifelong commitment you saw in your parents, grandparents, or another relative or friend. Talk about the meaningful legacy that you and your wife are seeking to carry on—or that you want to establish.

- Go out of your way to publicly honor and encourage other people's marriages.

- If you're divorced or separated, avoid bad-mouthing your children's mother. Cooperate with her and respect her wishes, even when your emotions tell you to do otherwise.

As a dad you have a great deal to say about your children's marriages and even the home lives of your yet-unborn grandchildren. But you can't dictate it or write it in a will. You have to model it.

MODEL A VITAL FAITH

Sadly, many fathers fail to spiritually equip their children. They may lead the family in prayers at meals or bedtime, but they leave most of the spiritual nurturing to Mom. After all, moms usually spend more time with the kids, and many are more naturally in tune with spiritual issues. But think about the potential danger of this. If boys grow up without a masculine model of spiritual vitality at home, they may be inclined to view Christianity as a feminine pursuit.

Gordon Dalbey has captured this well in his book *Healing the Masculine Soul.* He asserts that it isn't enough to tell men it's OK to be open and tender. We also need to "portray the manly strength and firmness that is of God."[2] We must show our sons that a life of obedience to Christ demonstrates the kind of strength that many men are hungering for: "toughness in the face of opposition, decisiveness in the face of uncertainty, and saving power in the face of danger."[3] We need to be living examples of a man who thinks for himself and celebrates the unique way God created him. At the same time, we need to be imitators of God.

Dad, if you understand who Jesus is, you know that He modeled *real* manhood: compassionate and strong, humble yet ready for action. That's the kind of sold-out faith your children need to see in you. Because, as you know, it takes courage to live for Christ in this unbelieving world. Your sons and daughters both need to see you live out your faith.

Our role as dads is to reveal by our lives that we are following another Role Model who is graciously and patiently completing His work in us (see Ephesians 2:10; Philippians 1:6; 1 Thessalonians 5:24). As we strive to be examples of humility, self-control, and grace in action, our children will see us walking our talk and will more likely choose to serve the Father.

And don't forget that it's good for your kids to know that you struggle sometimes—that you go through spiritual deserts and that you're not a super Christian. Remember, confessing your *inadequacies* makes you *adequate,* in part, to the task of spiritually equipping your children. When you are transparent, your observing children can look inside and see the gracious workings of the Spirit.

It is especially important to be open and vulnerable with teenagers. They already realize that you're not invincible, and they'll learn from watching your spiritual life: how you sin, but seek forgiveness; how you fail, but receive mercy; how you suffer, but find help. If they see how you are rescued from your failures, they'll better understand that their heavenly Father offers care and protection to each of His children. Whatever inadequacy you may feel as a dad should melt away as you begin to realize the power God has given you to be a living example of how much He loves you—and your children.

Most of all, if you want your children to imitate your faith, you will create an irresistible bond with them so that they are motivated not only by your example but even more by the depth and security of your relationship with them. Otherwise your kids may fight everything you stand for. That's what Sue did.

Her parents placed a high priority on training her in the faith. But as she matured into a teenager, she and her father gradually lost touch. During the week he was busy working—often traveling—and on weekends, church activities consumed much of his time. When her dad prayed before meals, Sue would stiffen. As she followed him into the church building on Sundays, she'd look at him with his holier-than-thou attitude and feel sick to her stomach. Some of that just happens with teenagers, but this was much more. Since her father's example wasn't backed up with a solid, caring relationship, Sue rebelled against his faith.

You've heard the saying: people don't care how much you know until they know how much you care. It's especially true among the "people" in your home. To pass along a sold-out trust in God, you have to focus on building a solid relationship with your kids. They need much more than a list of rules and principles. They need love to hold it all together.

MODEL EMOTIONAL MATURITY

Ron was in the backyard, cranking up his fourteen-year-old lawn mower. After so many years and so many repairs, the old beast just wouldn't start. Ron's frustration mounted. After cranking and cranking for several more minutes, he accidentally brushed his hand against the pull cord, which was so hot it burned him. Aggravated, he gave the mower a swift kick.

As he stood there stewing in emotion, he heard someone behind him. There was his two-year-old son, pushing his plastic lawn mower. Sure enough, the boy reared back and kicked that little mower, just like his dad.

As dads we need to help our children learn how to handle their emotions responsibly. Your children—especially your sons—are going to learn by watching you. How do you respond to crises, disagreements, and other stressful situations? Are you calm and positive, or do you sometimes lose your temper?

Many dads hide their emotions, perhaps thinking emotional displays are a sign of weakness. Maybe they were reared in homes where feelings were rarely discussed, certain topics were forbidden, and family members rarely said, "I'm sorry," or, "I love you."

Others have difficulty modeling consistency in moods, often because their own dads were inconsistent. They have not been able to order their emotional life, even as adults, because they've lacked a good reference point from which to draw a workable map of the emotional world. When they approached their own dad, they never knew whether he was going to hug them or belt them. Many of them grew up thinking that all fathers are emotionally distant.

But what is normal? Are a dad's sudden outbursts of anger typical to most fathers? Is that quick switch from affection to impatience a common thing? Definitely not.

Handling our emotions is not the same as *hiding* them or expressing them inappropriately. If we want to model godliness, we'll learn to express our emotions in healthy ways—whether we cry over a loss, maintain control during frustrations, or celebrate an achievement with a whoop and holler. Our kids need to see our emotions. They are a vital part of who we are. And even when we lose control and lash out at our kids in anger, we can turn our failure into something positive by going to our children, confessing that we were wrong, apologizing, and talking about better ways to handle emotions. Asking forgiveness is one of the most important things a dad can do. After all, humility is a characteristic of godliness.

MODEL INTEGRITY OF CHARACTER

Some years ago I purchased a dilapidated trailer to haul our family bikes for vacations and other expeditions. Then several summers later, I took that trailer to the local U-Haul to have some work done on the taillights for an upcoming trip.

About ten minutes after the mechanics started looking at the trailer, the manager of the store came out and informed me that the trailer I owned was stolen. We couldn't find a serial number, but sure enough, the design was just like an older model of U-Haul trailers that he showed me in a catalog. We scratched through several layers of paint and uncovered the trademark orange color of U-Haul. The man assured me that the company never sells used trailers to the public, so this had to be stolen.

Of course, when I came home and told my kids about this, they loved it. "Dad bought stolen goods!" But I knew they were watching me closely, wondering, *What's he going to do?* I weighed my options for a little bit. I really wanted to get on with the trip, but my better sense prevailed, and I knew I had to give up the trailer. Soon after I told my family this, the manager of the U-Haul store called and offered the use of one of his trailers—free of charge—for our trip. Thankfully, I made the right choice that day, and because I did my kids learned a powerful lesson: God takes care of you when you honor Him with your actions.

Remember, our values are *caught* more than *taught*. We can tell our kids how we want them to live. We can give them platitudes 'til we are blue in the face. But when we *show* them, the lesson really sticks.

Some time ago a father I know was wrestling with what some may consider an insignificant matter—wearing his seat belt. For years, he had only bothered wearing it when traveling several hours or on busy freeways. But then something significant and scary happened. His oldest child, a daughter, began driver's education classes at school. That's when he started wearing his seat belt every time he got in the car, recognizing that no matter what he tells his children, the life he lives communicates what he really believes. His desire to send a consistent message to them was important enough that he decided to make a permanent lifestyle change.

Dad, what are you modeling for your kids—through your action or inaction? Maybe a better question is, are you willing to make permanent lifestyle changes to ensure you're sending a consistent message? Is it too much to ask you to give up your favorite television show or to get rid of the radar detector?

These may not seem like big issues now, but what you do today will impact your children for years to come. Someday your son or daughter will be faced with important life decisions. How can your children defend truth if they haven't seen truth in action? When they are confronted with some wild philosophy at college, will they think, *What would my dad do?* and make a wise choice? Or will they think, *Well, Dad* said *this . . . but he usually* did *something else?*

As committed fathers, we should be very aware that our words and actions are being heard and watched. We're always on stage, and that awareness should add extra motivation to speak and act responsibly in a way that encourages and breathes life into those around us.

It's a good idea to regularly ask ourselves:

- What kind of example am I setting? My son is watching, and he needs to know what he should aspire to become.

- How does a "real man" act? My daughter is watching because she needs to know what to expect from men.

- My child's friends, teammates, and classmates—some of whom don't have a father at home—are also watching. What am I teaching them through what I say and how I live?

For the sake of our children and other kids in our spheres of influence, we need to be modeling healthy, genuine manhood. Children need a moral center, a place to anchor themselves. If we don't provide it, they may be left to drift on their own. They are depending on us to be models of integrity.

"AS HONEST AS THE DAY IS LONG ..."

When we consistently model godliness in our marriage, our faith, our emotions, and through our integrity, we will be that point of reference that can show our children how to outlive the world.

I'd like to close this chapter with one last story. Not long ago I had coffee with Clayton, who is in his seventies. I grabbed the opportunity to glean a nugget or two of wisdom from an elder and asked him, "What is the most valuable piece of insight you gained from your father or the character trait he modeled that has stuck with you?"

Clayton barely gave it a moment's thought: "Honesty," he said. "My father was as honest as the day is long. He taught me to be honest, too, and you know, sometimes it got me into trouble."

I had to hear more.

He continued, "One day I was in a high-level executive meeting with a CEO of the company and about a dozen other managers. The CEO always liked to share his ideas, and then the rest of us would take our turns talking about his tremendous insights. Everyone wanted to get on his good side, and of course he knew that.

"Well, on this day, after the CEO had voiced his opinions, I didn't like his idea, and I voiced a different opinion. I had to be honest; it's what my father taught me. When the CEO heard my response, he looked at everyone in the room and said, 'Well, I guess there's someone in here who's not looking for my job.'"

Well, Clayton never did become the CEO, but he didn't mind. He had his integrity, and that was much more valuable to him than wealth, status, or power.

Clayton's father had a visible and vocal commitment to honesty, and Clayton used his dad as a reference point for how to outlive the world. What greater reward could a father have?

MEETING THE CHALLENGE

Modeling

A father has a powerful influence on his children simply by displaying his character as part of his life. He knows what virtues he wants to encourage in his children, and he consciously demonstrates them daily. Above all, he practices what he preaches.

INSTRUCTIONS:

On a scale of 1 to 5, rank the accuracy of the following statements. Then add your scores and plot your total on the scale below. (You may want to have your child's mother or someone who knows you well take the survey and then compare their answers to yours. If your child no longer lives at home, score yourself as you remember your involvement.)

5 = Mostly True
4 = Somewhat True
3 = Undecided
2 = Somewhat False
1 = Mostly False

1. I demonstrate emotional maturity to my children. ☐

2. I am spiritually mature. ☐

3. I respond calmly when my children do something with which I disagree. ☐

4. I model behavior that I want my children to perform. ☐

5. I avoid habits or actions that I do not want my children doing. ☐

6. I am a good example to my children. ☐

TOTAL ☐

PLOT YOUR SCORE:

6	16	19	24	26	30
VERY POOR	POOR	AVERAGE	GOOD	VERY GOOD	

(The scale is not uniform because it is based on norms from a study of 1,516 fathers.)

QUESTIONS FOR DISCUSSION AND REFLECTION

As you consider how you scored on modeling, think about the following questions and discuss them with some other fathers..

1. What specific character traits or virtues did your father model for you?

2. Who has influenced the example you're seeking to set for your children? Specifically, how have you been influenced?

3. When are children most impressionable to their father's example?

4. In your opinion, what are three of the most destructive influences on your child's behavior?

5. What other resources are available to reinforce the values, lifestyle, and behavior you're seeking to model?

ACTION POINTS

Choose one of the following action points and commit to doing it before you go on to the next chapter (or your next group meeting).

1. Think of one or two habits or virtues you'd like your children to develop as they mature. Come up with specific ways you can model those attributes.

2. Do something you have been promising your kids.

3. Take your kids to do yard work for an elderly person.

4. Discuss with your wife some of the negative modeling your children are receiving from friends, peers, the media, or from you.

5. Take a hard look at your daily habits and emotions. Is there

room for improvement? Have you been giving your integrity enough thoughtful consideration?

6. Make sure you pick up your clothes and keep your room tidy.

7. When the car or a major appliance breaks down, show your children how to handle the problem positively.

8. Explain to your children why you have voted for a particular candidate instead of another.

9. Always be extra considerate of your wife. Help her with tasks around the house; hold doors open for her; compliment her in your children's presence.

10. Ask your children often: "How can I help?"

CHAPTER 9

FOSTER SELF-CONTROL

Train a child in the way he should go, and when he is old, he will not turn from it.

PROVERBS 22:6

In his best-selling book *The 7 Habits of Highly Effective Families*, Stephen Covey tells the following story. A father and mother were at their wit's end in regard to their daughter. Her behavior was irresponsible and disrespectful, and things were only going south. Clearly, they had to do something before the daughter's behavior tore the family apart.

One day they decided that when she came home that evening, they'd give her an ultimatum. She would make certain changes or she would move out. As they waited for their daughter, the dad took a sheet of paper and began to list the changes she'd have to make in order to stay. It was an excruciating experience since he couldn't imagine that she'd agree to the changes he was demanding.

Then, as he continued to wait, something prompted him to turn the page over and make another list. This time, he wrote down some of the things *he* would change if his daughter agreed to the items on the other side. When he finished, he was in tears. His list of changes was longer than the one he'd made for his daughter.

When she did eventually come home—because of his broken, humble spirit—their talk was heartfelt and meaningful. Why? Because the dad began the conversation by going through the items on *his* side of the paper, not hers. He wanted to change. His daughter saw his sincerity, and she was more open to making changes herself.[1]

This wise dad understood that all children will test their father's patience and that all children need a dad who's approachable and accepting, who listens to his children's concerns and remains open to their ideas, who's slow to anger, and who seldom overreacts. He was creating an environment that nurtures *self-control.*

Dads, if we want our children to grow up to be confident, self-controlled adults who make wise choices, take responsibility for their actions, and proactively work to fix their own problems, we will seek to foster self-control in them by monitoring them, being an example of self-control, extolling the benefits of sexual purity, and providing correction. Let's take a closer look at each of these.

MONITOR YOUR KIDS

Did you know that your children need you to look over their shoulder . . . keep them in check . . . hold them accountable? Your first thought may be that you don't want to *interfere* in your child's life. In our culture, interference means being overbearing or controlling. But think of it this way: Is it wrong to tell your three-year-old to back away from the edge of a cliff? Is it wrong to teach your son, the new driver, about watching for cars in his blind spot? One of our most important roles as a father is to caution and teach our children about decisions and consequences. A proactive, "interfering" father will know what his kids are being exposed to in the classroom, in the locker room, and with his friends.

This is particularly critical for sons. When boys and young men aren't monitored in a healthy way and given the correction they need, they are far less likely to develop self-control and more likely to become involved in gangs, sexual activity that often leads to unwanted pregnancies, and crime.

We see an example of this in 1 Kings 1. King David has been renowned as a ruler and a man after God's own heart, but he struggled as a father. As the story goes, his sons were quarreling over the right to become the next king. In fact, Adonijah, his fourth son, had already proclaimed his right to succession. Adonijah's attempt failed. Verse 6 tells us that "his father had never interfered with him by asking, 'Why do you behave as you do?'" (NIV). Clearly, David failed to provide active discipline and guidance for his son Adonijah. In addition, two of David's other sons, Absalom and Amnon, died because their lifestyles led them down roads of immorality and rebellion rather than integrity and justice.

Dad, don't let your kids go off the deep end. Let them know you're watching them and that you're not going to stand by and allow them to disregard God's Word. For example, don't let your kids talk trash, curse, tell coarse jokes, or denigrate others. It's the parents' job to teach kids to be respectful and to use their speech for positive ends, such as articulating thoughts and feelings, building relationships, giving encouragement, and speaking words of life and peace. If we stand by and let dishonesty or disobedience go on, then we can expect the natural consequences of these actions to become worse and worse. Children need to know that they have boundaries and that you're going to be there to confront them when they step out of line.

You can also help your children develop self-control by modeling it. As we pointed out in the last chapter, your actions speak much louder than your words.

BE AN EXAMPLE OF SELF-CONTROL

We've all seen—or perhaps grown up under—a "formula father," who goes too far with control. He demands perfect order and obedience, and there is wrath to pay for the child who steps outside his boundaries or gets on his nerves. We may also be familiar with the other extreme, the "freewheeling father." He knows there are no guarantees with children anyway, so why worry so much about discipline? Some of these dads adopt the view that we should never upset our children in any way or deny them something they want. Where's the happy medium? How do we teach our kids responsibility and self-control without losing control ourselves?

Two of the Bible's most pointed statements to fathers are:

Fathers, do not exasperate your children; instead, bring them up in the training and instruction of the Lord. (Ephesians 6:4 NIV)

Fathers, do not embitter your children, or they will become discouraged. (Colossians 3:21 NIV)

When we exasperate our children, it's as if we have sucked the air out of them. They are at their wit's end. We could exasperate our daughter when, after working hard, she brings home an 85 percent on an assignment, and we're not satisfied. We could exasperate our son when we go overboard and nag him about his grammar or his slackness in keeping his room clean, or we place high expectations on him that he can't possibly fulfill. We may continue harping on a child long after we've made a point or focus on correction at a time when he or she needs encouragement.

We may embitter our children by making a promise and never fulfilling it or by doing something hurtful and failing to come back and ask that child for forgiveness. We can embitter our kids when we make flippant, everyday comments or unkind, sarcastic jokes that discourage rather than build them up or by showing more interest in our own agenda than in what a child is thinking or feeling.

Do you recognize yourself in any of these behaviors? I know I have done some of these things and have been committed to change so that I model the self-control I want my children to develop.

While studying the qualities of effective fathers, I noticed a trend in the data. Along with my colleague Dr. Gale Roid, I identified a "calmness factor" that distinguishes fathering using four factors. CALM dads are:

Consistent. They don't change like the weather; their moods and behaviors are predictable and steady. You can rely on their word, and their children know what to expect from them. They also respond positively and calmly during crises or other stressful times.

Aware. Calm dads are alert to the developmental issues, desires, needs, and circumstances their children are dealing with. They know when a child is upset or has had a tough day. This awareness guides the expectations they have for each child, ensuring that they are reasonable, and motivates them to give each child individual time and attention.

Listeners. Calm fathers listen without interrupting, and they give their children plenty of freedom to express themselves.

They listen carefully and don't lose it when a child says something off the wall. They're patient with mistakes.

M*odels*. They demonstrate the behaviors they hope their children will emulate, including a willingness to be humble and seek forgiveness for any wrongdoing. They point out mature, praiseworthy conduct in others.

Though the Bible does not explicitly link fathering with calmness, it provides this powerful picture of God as a loving Father to the people of Israel: "I led them with cords of human kindness, with ties of love; I lifted the yoke from their neck and bent down to feed them" (Hosea 11:4 NIV). And though the people of Israel turned away from Him, He said, "I will not carry out my fierce anger, nor will I turn and devastate Ephraim. . . . I will not come in wrath" (v. 9).

Scripture often exhorts us to live a confident, selfless, peaceful, trust-filled way of life. For example:

Man's anger does not bring about the righteous life that God desires. (James 1:20 NIV)

The fruit of the Spirit is love, joy, peace, patience, kindness, goodness, faithfulness, gentleness and self-control. (Galatians 5:22–23)

At times in Jesus's life, He expressed anger and outrage, but it was always directed toward a higher purpose, and He was never angry with children. He was tender, compassionate, and self-controlled. We need to be the same. And we need to encourage self-control in our children, particularly in the area of sex.

EXTOL THE VIRTUES OF SEXUAL PURITY

If we want our children to learn and exercise self-control in this key area, if we want them to have a healthy, God-centered view of sexuality, we need to be proactive in educating them about sex and sexual purity. We must be open, honest, and ready to talk, whether we're laying out the biological facts or going deeper into issues, such as pornography or our own areas of struggle.

Believe me, your children want your input in this area—even if they are too embarrassed to ask you about it outright. When it comes to sex, one of the deepest needs of most teenagers is to understand their budding sexuality. They're curious. Their hormones are kicking in, and they want to know how to respond. What is good? What is normal? They pick up some clues from friends. They may watch television or listen to the radio and take subconscious notes.

Another reason some teenagers experiment with sex is to fill their deep, unfulfilled need for love, touch, and intimacy. Daughters especially need a tender, heart-to-heart connection with their dads, and if they don't experience that, they may go looking for it elsewhere. That was true for nineteen-year-old Wendy. She was involved in a tangled, unhealthy relationship with her boyfriend. Her biological dad was a brick wall when it came to communicating his feelings about her. As a consequence, she always questioned her inner beauty and sense of worth. Wendy's stepfather, on the other hand, constantly

> Hardly any behavioral trait in boys or girls is more valued by parents in these hectic, every-moment-accounted-for days than self-control.[2]
>
> DR. KYLE PRUETT

berated her. He ripped into her about her weight, her attitudes, and her feelings. It's easy to see how her relationship with her boyfriend is a misguided attempt to find intimacy and acceptance.

Dad, you can help meet those needs. Show your children healthy affection and initiate conversations that help them understand why God reserves sex for marriage. Visit the topic early and often, and let your kids know you're available for any questions they may have. It may seem awkward, but make sure they know you care and that you aren't just saying this because you feel obligated.

Here's an overview of what you need to cover:

1. *Present the pertinent facts and let them know how to respond to challenging situations.* A little research will help you be age-appropriate and keep you from leaving out something important. In addition, with sexual abuse cases on the rise, young children need to be told that no one is allowed to touch any part of their body that their swimsuit touches— and that if someone does, they need to tell you or an authority immediately.

2. *Convey God's plan for love, romance, and sex within the commitment of marriage.* Teach them what the Bible says about temptation, lust, purity, and fidelity. For example:

   • In the midst of his desperate suffering, Job writes that he has made a covenant with his eyes not to look lustfully on a woman (see Job 31:1).

   • "Let the marriage bed be undefiled" (Hebrews 13:4)— speaking of the sexual aspect of marriage and God's desire for sex to be reserved for husband and wife.

   • Proverbs 5, 6, and 7 are full of admonitions to young men to keep their ways pure. "Do not lust in your heart after [the immoral woman] or let her captivate you with her eyes, for the prostitute reduces you to a loaf of bread, and the adulteress preys upon your very life" (Proverbs 6:25–26 NIV).

- "The body is not meant for sexual immorality, but for the Lord, and the Lord for the body" (1 Corinthians 6:13 NIV).

The Old Testament provides both positive and negative examples about how to handle sexual temptation. David and Samson both struggled to keep their sexual lives in order and were thrown off course with God because they lost control sexually (see 2 Samuel 11–12 and Judges 13–16). But when Potiphar's wife tried to seduce Joseph, he ran away—naked even—because he knew he couldn't compromise his service to his boss, and most of all, his service to God (see Genesis 39).

Study these scriptural admonitions—in an appropriate time and way—with your children. But study them in this context: "I, too, heed these directives as a father; these are the scriptures I cling to as a safeguard in my own life." Share these biblical stories with your kids so they can see the connection between a person's disobedience to God and the negative consequences that follow.

3. *Make sure your children are well acquainted with all the good reasons to save themselves for marriage.* Here are some reasons to start you thinking:

- Sex outside marriage gives only the illusion of intimacy. Premarital sex preoccupies a dating relationship while bypassing all the hard work of communication necessary for genuine intimacy.

- Genuine intimacy—which someone has defined as "into-me-see"—grows out of the hard work of getting to know your date, sharing goals, building trust, and holding each other accountable.

- Sexual promiscuity can create unhealthy patterns that short-circuit sexual enjoyment with your future spouse. Spouses who have been sexually active will bring their history into the marriage, and that can breed doubt and insecurity in the other partner. Conversely, those who remain virgins—not just technically, but in the truest sense—have already proven their character, their maturity, and their self-control, which thus builds trust within marriage.

- Physical involvement prior to marriage, even backrubs and light kissing, tends to follow the law of diminishing returns, meaning that each time a couple gets together, they have to go further and further. One night's level of pleasure is just not as satisfying the next time around, and so the pressure builds to "go all the way," and often that pressure can be transferred to other partners.

- The emotional high promised by pop culture is a lie. Instead, premarital sexual activity leaves us vulnerable to a host of destructive emotions—suspicion, guilt, stress, emptiness, jealousy, and so on.

- Sexual intercourse outside of marriage not only leads to emotional distress but also to unplanned pregnancies and dozens of sexually transmitted diseases, including AIDS—even while using a contraceptive.

- God's standards for leaving, cleaving, and becoming one

flesh (see Genesis 2:24 KJV) are designed to maximize the joy of sex within marriage.

4. *Prepare your son for how he will be tempted in this area.* Alluring images assault us from everywhere, and you need to prepare him for the battle. Tell him exactly what to expect; talk through scenarios where he'll be tempted; read together from 1 Corinthians 6:18 about fleeing from sexual immorality. Help him plan the right choice now—before he finds himself in a difficult situation. Talk about how he can channel his sexual drive in healthy ways, such as exercise. Encourage him to pray daily for strength—and you pray for his purity as well. Sexual passion is a good gift of God, but it's important that we protect that gift and see that it isn't polluted or stained by the world (see James 1).

5. *Tell your older kids about some of your own struggles in this area and what you learned in the process.* As your children mature, tell them how God led you out of temptation or perhaps delivered you from a decadent lifestyle. Share any consequence you suffered, what you learned, and your hopes for them in this area. Above all, remind them that it's something you have to address and pray about daily because temptations are everywhere.

And don't forget to continue to affirm your sons and daughters for who they are and how God created them. Your love and support will give them the confidence and anchor they need to exercise self-control in this critical area of their lives.

Along with modeling and teaching self-control, dads who want to foster self-control in their kids will provide needed discipline and correction.

PROVIDE DISCIPLINE AND CORRECTION

What is the purpose of corrective discipline? That's a question to consider when we're not in the middle of a discipline situation! Too many parents discipline by the seat of their pants, so to speak. They don't make decisions about discipline until something happens and they need to deal with a child. And by then they're usually frustrated and angry and less than patient.

I believe that Proverbs 3:11–12 speaks directly to this issue: "My son, do not despise the LORD's discipline and do not resent his rebuke, because the LORD disciplines those he loves, as a father the son he delights in" (NIV). We don't often connect *love* and *delight* with discipline, but we should.

Our loving hopes for our children motivate us to discipline them when they do wrong and to protect them. Life places numerous pitfalls in their paths: a hot stove, a too-friendly stranger, an opportunity to cheat on an exam, a classmate with drugs. Through the protection of discipline, we can avoid being "a willing party to [their] death" (Proverbs 19:18 NIV), whether the threat is physical, emotional, or spiritual. Some have described healthy correction as *rescuing* our children from the danger that comes with a life of disrespect and disobedience. Positive discipline is done out of love and leads to hope.

Discipline is not just about influencing right behavior. It's an expression of affection and nurturance. And that makes sense since discipline and nurturance actually have the same goal: helping our children become confident, well-adjusted people who will outlive the world. Our children will likely be more motivated toward right behavior through our expression of our love for them and hope for their future than by our threats. A close bond with a child is perhaps the greatest asset we have when it comes to correcting him.

Discipline encompasses all our interactions with our children—training, shaping, and encouraging them. But the toughest part of discipline is changing behavior—enforcing limits, carrying out consequences, holding children accountable for their actions. Often, our methods work against that goal.

I will present some basic guidelines here, but I recommend that you talk with your wife and come up with a more specific plan that takes into account your own strengths and weaknesses, your feelings about discipline, and your children's unique traits and temperaments.

For example, how do you and your wife feel about spanking? Some parents are appalled at the thought of bringing physical pain to a child. Others see spanking as a difficult, but necessary, way to correct their children. In my experience, it requires time and patience to make spanking an effective method of discipline. Many parents spank or have been spanked in unhealthy ways—in anger or frustration or using an inconsistent standard, and this is harmful. But I believe God's Word teaches that spanking is a legitimate tool for training children—when done with love and hope and integrating prayer. But it should not be the only form of discipline you use, and any discipline should be followed by a time of talking and listening and healing the relationship with the child.

On to a few basic principles:

1. *Use the Bible as your reference for proper behavior.* What kind of behavior should you expect from your children?

Sit down with your wife and discuss the actions and attitudes God sees as unacceptable. Start with the Ten Commandments and add to the list. I recommend putting defiance and disrespect at the top of your list. Also think about the principles involved, not just the behavior. For example, telling a lie is a pretty big no-no at our house. But dishonesty is the bigger principle, because that includes deceit, lies of omission, and the issue of integrity.

2. *Communicate clearly about expectations, limits, and consequences.* Children want to know what's expected of them, what happens when they don't do what's expected, and who's going to enforce the rules. Your children will find a way to take advantage of anything that's vague or unspecified. For example, if you say, "Son, please take out the trash," you are leaving him room to do it when, where, and however *he* wants to. And chances are, your ideas of when and how are different from his. Instead, tell him. Be clear, and make sure your child acknowledges the details of what you have said.

It may seem easier to solve the immediate problem by yelling at our children or punishing them, but we do our best fatherly teaching and training when we slow down, ask, "why?" and make the effort to help our children become responsible adults.

3. *When they have willfully disobeyed, don't let them out of the consequences.* Your kids need to know that you mean what you say. If they understand that when they're still in diapers, they'll remember it when they get their driver's license. With consequences, children have to understand

and admit that they did something wrong; the punishment has to fit the offense, it has to be meaningful and age-appropriate, and it shouldn't be a long, drawn-out process. If they gripe and complain, that's when you know it's working! Just make sure the consequences rest on their shoulders. That's how they learn about responsibility and the consequences of real-life decisions.

Now, I know that might sound too easy. What if an older child throws out all he's been taught in favor of some very destructive or immoral ideals? I know how invested you are in your child, but you cannot rescue him at this point if he has set his face toward destructive behavior. If there are irreconcilable differences, you have to live your life based on your own values. Repeated conflicts aren't healthy for anyone. Do what you know is best for him and for your family, even if it means taking a "tough love" stand. Continue to exercise the virtue of self-control. Don't try to rescue your child, but neither should you violently expel him. Let him know your door is always open, continue to pray with patience, and take heart. In many cases, a wayward child will return.

Most teenagers will question at least some of the premises on which their parents have built their lives. It's part of the independence they are establishing. So don't be shocked if yours go out of their way to express their different views of politics, religion, or other values you hold dear. Instead of giving lectures or making demands, focus on seeking to understand your teens and keeping an open dialogue. Try not to get too emotional, and continue to show respect and love. Pray for them, and look for ways to be a positive influence.

4. *Show empathy, not anger.* A dad who shows empathy and sadness instead of anger can help his children learn from their mistakes instead of getting caught up in anger, frustration, and resentment. If your first response to misbehavior is empathy, you can short-circuit your anger and avoid a meltdown. It's easier on us, and it's actually harder on our kids, because now they have to work on solving the problem. And it's far more respectful.

   If you feel uncontrollable anger building when you are correcting a child, give yourself a time-out. Tell your child you'll deal with the situation later, which will give you time to think about it and talk it over with the child's mother. Then turn on soothing music, take a short walk, get some fresh air, even do some push-ups or jumping jacks to let off steam; pray.

5. *Work as a team with your wife and other authority figures in your children's lives.* This is essential in the area of expectations and discipline. Kids need to see a consistent purpose behind what their parents do. Discuss any disagreements later, in private. You can always go back to your children together and say, "We talked it over, and we didn't handle this in the best way." Then take whatever steps are appropriate. Kids are clever: if the two of you aren't united, they'll find ways to exploit the situation and pit you against each other, and that only multiplies the problems. But a mom and dad who appreciate each other's unique

approach and learn to work together will bring great blessings to their kids.

6. *Keep demonstrating your love.* We need to let our children clearly know that, though their behavior may be unacceptable, we will always love and accept them as our children. Even in discipline, we can still be gentle—demonstrating love and care.

Maybe the best way to view corrective discipline is that—as a parent—you're doling out small doses of consequences now for small infractions so that later your son or daughter doesn't have to face huge consequences for huge infractions. When you look at it that way, discipline is really a very loving and hope-driven thing to do.

A TWO-WAY STREET

If things are tense between you and your children, it can create a barrier to their growth and confidence and may counteract your attempts to teach them self-control. Some creative, courageous, loving action may be in order, and a confession or apology may be a good place to start. You might need to say something like, "Katie, I know I've been busy in my own world recently, and I'm sorry." Depending on her response, you may be able to go a little deeper: "So, I'd like to know, what's going on in *your* world that may have left you a little worried or stressed?" Or, maybe you should just come right out and ask, "Is there anything I can do to help strengthen our relationship?"

Though they may not admit it, your children want to connect with you. They need you to encourage them in their goals and pursuits and validate them as beloved children. But don't expect perfection. They will fail sometimes, even in their relationships. When they do, show them grace and find common ground.

MEETING THE CHALLENGE

Maintaining Self-Control

A calm father knows how to maintain his composure in the heat of the battle. He can see beyond the immediate crisis and keep long-term goals in focus. His responses to his children's needs are consistent, thoughtful, and reasonable.

INSTRUCTIONS:

On a scale of 1 to 5, rank the accuracy of the following statements. Then add your scores and plot your total on the scale below. (You may want to have your child's mother or someone who knows you well take the survey and then compare their answers to yours. If your child no longer lives at home, score yourself as you remember your involvement.)

5 = Mostly True
4 = Somewhat True
3 = Undecided
2 = Somewhat False
1 = Mostly False

1. I am able to discuss differences in my family. ☐

2. I am able to respond calmly when my children say hurtful things to me. ☐

3. I am patient with my children when they make mistakes. ☐

4. I do not lose my temper with my children. ☐

5. I respond calmly when my children do something with which I do not agree. ☐

6. I am levelheaded during a crisis. ☐

TOTAL ☐

PLOT YOUR SCORE:

6	16	19	24	27	30
VERY POOR	POOR	AVERAGE	GOOD	VERY GOOD	

(The scale is not uniform because it is based on norms from a study of 1,516 fathers.)

QUESTIONS FOR DISCUSSION AND REFLECTION

As you consider how you scored on this inventory, think about the following questions and discuss them with some other fathers.

1. Was your father a calming presence in your life?

2. How do you typically respond when a family member hurls a hurtful comment at you?

3. When is the last time you asked for forgiveness from another family member?

4. How do you demonstrate and model calmness to your children?

5. How do you express emotion in your household?

ACTION POINTS

Choose one of the following action points and commit to doing it before you go on to the next chapter (or your next group meeting).

1. Ask your wife to help you identify when your tone of voice becomes harsh when talking to your children and what effect it has on them.

2. Do a priority self-check using Dr. Richard Swenson's three important rules about values: "The first is that people are more important than things. The second is that people are more important than things. And the third is that people are more important than things."[3]

3. At the dinner table, tell each child a positive quality you've noticed in him or her.

4. When disciplining your children, always be sure to explain

why their behavior is wrong and provide affirmation and restoration afterward.

5. When your children are speaking to you, be sure to remove any distractions—television, newspaper, computer, and so on—that might discourage them from talking or hinder you from understanding.

6. Be willing to admit when you've been wrong or harsh with your child. Practice these words: "I was wrong. I'm sorry. Will you forgive me?"

7. Plan a healthy, positive response for the next time you are angry with your children.

8. Examine your behavior at your children's sports events and ask your family to let you know when you're out of line.

CHAPTER 10

BUILD A GODLY LEGACY

A good man leaves an inheritance for his children's children.

PROVERBS 13:22 NIV

Several years ago Milton Siegel's mother gave him a small, black notebook that she had found in a box of things that had belonged to her parents, Milton's grandparents. When he opened the notebook, it took on special meaning for him. It had belonged to his grandfather, James Lynn, who had died before Milton met him. Milton never knew much about his grandfather, but the notebook provided some important clues.

Upon opening it, Milton saw that his grandfather had typed a few special Bible verses in it. The typing was far from perfect. Some of the scriptures were typed at a slant across the pages, and mistakes had been corrected with a pencil or a pen. "But that wasn't important," Milton says. "What was important to me was that in the 1930s or '40s, my grandfather had taken the time to type these Bible verses in the notebook. As I learned later, he carried the notebook with him wherever he went, and now I do the same thing. I carry that small, plain notebook with me in my briefcase, and sometimes, when I am traveling, I take out the notebook and thumb through the brittle pages, reflecting on the verses and my grandfather's faith.

"Eventually, I'll pass along the small, black notebook to my son or daughter. Years from now, a grandchild who is not yet born—or perhaps even a great-grandchild—will be given the small, black notebook and grow stronger in his or her faith because of this seemingly insignificant notebook."[1]

I get excited by such stories, and I think we can all learn something from Milton. A godly legacy can be a powerful source of encouragement and strength in the lives of our children and grandchildren. Just as his grandfather's notebook did for Milton, it may turn them toward their heavenly Father.

Dad, make it your goal to leave a godly legacy. Keep an eternal perspective. Effective fathering is primarily about having our priorities straight, reaffirming them every day, and then taking action based on those priorities. When you leave a godly legacy, you will continue to have an impact on others, long after you have died. This is one way each of us can truly outlive the world.

> The only things that really matter when your life is over are: who you loved, who loved you, and what you did together to serve God.[2]
>
> JAMES DOBSON

If our kids see us outliving the world in this way, they will be more likely to rear their own children to outlive the world, as well, as will future generations. When it's our goal to leave a godly legacy, we will view life from an eternal perspective, and our lives will make a difference for generations to come.

But before we talk more about the legacy we leave behind, let's take a closer look at the legacy we received from our fathers and grandfathers.

BREAK ANY DESTRUCTIVE PATTERNS YOU INHERITED

In chapter 1, I highlighted the importance of making peace with our fathering past and finding healing, if necessary. Why? Because the past impacts our future. Let me give you a lighthearted illustration of this truth.

When my oldest son, Joel, was a teenager, he took the family vehicle out for a little expedition. He was off-roading in the Kansas fields near a pond, and the car got stuck. Actually, the word *stuck* is too mild—the tires were buried up to the fenders in mud. Joel and his friends spent six hours working furiously to get the car out of the mud, to no avail. The next day, I spent hours digging and working on it, as well, and finally brought it home. But first, of course, I took pictures.

Several days later we were with my parents, and I brought the photos along to share the event. As Joel was showing the pictures to his grandfather, I noticed my dad just smiling. I asked him why, and then it came out. Some six decades earlier, when he was sixteen, he had done the same thing. He had been driving across a lake bed and his car got buried in mud. He, too, had to call his dad to bail him out. When we heard the story, we couldn't help but laugh—even Joel.

I share this story because it shows the power of generational linkage. The behaviors and values of the generations that came before us trickle down and have an impact on us.

Exodus 34:7 describes how the sins of fathers can show up in their children to the third or fourth generation, and I have often observed this in families. A behavior from one generation shows up—sometimes surprisingly—one or even two generations later. If a father struggles with addictions or has a string of unsuccessful marriages, that legacy will often haunt his children and grandchildren. Sometimes those sins aren't just passed on but multiplied in the following generations. And when that sin is out-of-control anger or substance abuse or even child abuse, it's tragic and shameful.

Take some time to evaluate the legacy you inherited. Reflect on what happened in your life before you became a father, including how you related to your own father. It's important to do this, because the present and future are critically linked to the past.

As you think about your relationship to your father or father figure, consider these questions:

- How would you describe his support of you?
- Did he regularly show you affection?
- Was he present and accessible to you growing up?
- Did he struggle with substance abuse, or was he unfaithful to your mother?
- Did he abuse you or another family member?
- Would you say he was a good example?

If, like many of us, you received a less-than-ideal legacy, God can enable you to break the power of generational sin. There is hope for healing. Jeremiah writes of a new day when "people will no longer say, 'The fathers have eaten sour grapes and the children's teeth are set on edge.' Instead, everyone will die for his own sin; whoever eats sour grapes—his own teeth will be set on edge" (Jeremiah 31:29–30 NIV). And God says His blessings will extend to a thousand generations of those who love Him and keep His commands (see Deuteronomy 5:10).

Bob's story is a beacon of hope to all who wrestle with generational sin. His dad, grandfather, and great-grandfather were all alcoholics. When Bob's dad wasn't drunk and tired, his method of dealing with the world was to verbally abuse Bob and other members of the family. Bob's dad often told his son, "You can't do anything right!" Bob sometimes saw his father slap his mom or shove her against a counter at the end of an argument.

One day when Bob was ten years old, he climbed up into a tree near their house after one of his father's tirades. Perched between two branches, he watched his father come out of the house and get into his '55 Buick. As his dad turned the key and began to pull out of the driveway, Bob yelled, "I hate you! I wish you were dead! I wish you were dead!"

Little did Bob know, he would soon get his wish. Two hours later, his father was in a car accident that ended his life. Bob's last words to his father haunted him for many years.

When Bob grew up, he, too, became an alcoholic. When he eventually married and became a father, he treated his family just like his own father had treated him. Unhappy with his life and who he was, Bob began a pilgrimage that led him into a deep spiritual faith and an end to his drinking. Still, his feelings toward his father were unresolved.

Then one night, Bob had a vivid dream. The same images that had haunted him his entire life returned: he was sitting in a tree, looking out over the driveway, watching his father get into the '55 Buick. But this time the event did not repeat itself. Instead, Bob walked closer to the car and looked into the driver's-side window. The man behind the wheel turned his face toward Bob, but it wasn't his father. It was Jesus. He rolled down the window, looked Bob right in the eyes and said, "Get in, Bob. It's OK. You can ride with me."

That dream carried great significance for Bob, and that night signaled a turning point. You could say Bob placed his life in the car from that point on. He let Jesus drive, if you will, and gradually overcame the pain in his past and the cycle of alcoholism in his family. Through a long process spanning several years, Bob let go, accepted God's forgiveness for what he'd said to his father, and in time he became the father his four children needed.

Today Bob is a healed healer. Though unique and extraordinary, his story represents how God can heal addicted, irresponsible men and transform them into effective fathers. The cycle of abuse and alcoholism has been broken, freeing not only Bob, but also his children and grandchildren.

That new day can come for all fathers. When a man effectively fathers, he purposely and resolutely breaks a pattern that he knows has been less than ideal. It's a brave moment, designed to thrill a man's heart. I know, because this has been my experience. My own father wasn't allowed to be there when I was born, and I've been told that he didn't really become involved in many aspects of my life until I was two or three years old. But when my daughter Hannah was born, I was in a constant state of amazement at what God had entrusted to me as her father. As I spent hours holding her—talking to her, walking with her, changing her diaper—I found healing for the confusion I'd felt about how my own father had reacted to me as a child.

Every father is imperfect, so all of us are wounded in some large or small way. Do you know God as your Abba Father? The Scriptures tell us He is ready and eager to give you good gifts. You can keep your children from the clutches of the curse as you demonstrate your God-given father power and help them outlive the world by passing on a godly legacy.

BE INTENTIONAL ABOUT YOUR LEGACY

Each of us needs to think every day about the legacy we are creating. Thoughts of our legacy, our place in history, and what we leave our children should be ever present in our minds. Often, during the early years of fatherhood, we're so busy with the details of life—establishing ourselves in a career, meeting our family's daily needs, or just trying to keep up with our energetic youngsters—that any long-term thoughts of our fathering heritage get clouded over. As we mature and enter our forties, fifties, and sixties, the clouds lift and the question of our legacy emerges.

Is your life reflecting what's important to you? Look over the past year of your life and consider the following questions:

1. How did you invest the bulk of your time with your family?

2. Did you pursue the things that were really important to your relationships?

3. What was the biggest obstacle that kept you from doing with your family what was on your heart?

4. What is one important goal you have for them for this coming year?

Whether you're a father, a grandfather, or a father figure, you have tremendous influence and power—probably more than you realize. You have the power to strengthen the next generation or destroy it. Your invisible presence will be felt for decades. If that presence is negative, it may take years for your descendants to process the pain and find healing. If that presence is positive, you will become a solid point of reference by which your children can measure the universe.

But you can't build a godly legacy without being intentional about it. It's a step-by-step process that requires long-range planning and daily investments. So if you want to be a purposeful dad of destiny . . .

1. *Do some research and reminiscing.* Imagine yourself at the end of your life. How do you want your kids and future generations to remember you? As a hard worker? A humorous dad? Someone who was always there for them? A man of sincere and active faith?

   What kind of legacy do you want to leave future generations? Take some time to answer this question—it's worth pondering—and keep in mind the following questions:

   • What values and skills do you want to pass on to your children?

   • What are your children's greatest challenges?

   • What are their greatest strengths and gifts?

   • How can you strengthen your relationship with your children in the coming year?

   • What physical and emotional resources will be required for your children to face the future with confidence?

   • Whom can you count on for support and counsel as you father your children?

   Take your time answering these questions. Talk them over with your wife or someone who knows you well.

   Consider making a list of the values, skills, and ideals that are important for you to transmit. If you aren't sure how to answer that question, ask an older father what legacy he hopes to leave for his children and what he is doing specifically to accomplish that. Write down all that priceless information.

2. *Pray about all you've recorded and start sharing those things with your children.* Talk with your children about your values and what you hope to instill in them. Talk about your dreams for them and how you hope they live their lives.

3. *Leave a written legacy.* Write down your thoughts about life, and tailor them to each child personally. This can be a tangible reminder to future generations that you were serious about your faith, just as his grandfather's little black notebook was to Milton Siegel.

You might include childhood experiences that shaped who you are; your perspective on education; your attitudes toward the opposite sex; your thoughts on character, purity, godliness, and marriage. Chart out your faith journey and view of God. Write about your struggles, fears, and failures, as well as your successes and victories, dreams and passions. Do it now while you have the opportunity.

4. *Look for ways to extend your legacy.* God may be preparing you to have an unexpected impact in the life of a boy or girl outside your family. That was the case for Esther, whose parents had both died (see Esther 2:7). Her uncle, a godly man named Mordecai, took her in as his own daughter. He invested himself in her, and God did great things through her—and ultimately through Mordecai. When Mordecai uncovered a conspiracy to kill the king,

he told Esther about it and she was able to warn the king—her husband—and save his life (2:22). And when the king's right-hand man, Haman, convinced the king to kill all the Jews, Mordecai convinced Esther to plead for the lives of her people, even at the risk of losing her own life. He told her: "Do not think that because you are in the king's house you alone of all the Jews will escape. For if you remain silent at this time, relief and deliverance for the Jews will arise from another place, but you and your father's family will perish. And who knows but that you have come to royal position for such a time as this?" (4:13–14 NIV). Because of Mordecai's example and influence, Esther was able to save the Jews from destruction.

Dad, focus your efforts on lasting values and people instead of on temporal things, such as possessions, career advancement, or leisure pursuits. Jesus said, "A man's life does not consist in the abundance of his possessions" (Luke 12:15 NIV). We weren't made to collect DVDs or motorcycles or power tools or even to build a financial legacy. We need to enjoy our kids and invest in them; they're among God's greatest gifts to us. True joy comes from loving, connected relationships with God and with people. That's why He created us.

"I WOULDN'T TRADE HIM FOR ALL THE DADS IN THE WORLD"

I'd like to close this chapter with a story about the legacy of a grandfather who stood in the gap. During one of our National Center for Fathering essay contests, we received this winning entry from nine-year-old Jordan:

The dad in my life isn't really my dad, he's my Grandpa. But he's been like a dad to me. Four months before I was born, my real father left my mommy.

Grandpa drove 400 miles to come get my mommy and me and brought us back to Minnesota. He took care of my mommy until I was born. When I came home from the hospital, there was a cradle that Grandpa made just for me. Someday, my kids will sleep in the same cradle.

When I was a baby, I cried a lot at night. Grandpa would walk me around and around the kitchen table. He rocked me to sleep, and he was my first baby-sitter. Now I'm nine years old, and Grandpa is my best buddy. We do lots of things together. We go to zoos, museums, and parks. We watch baseball games on TV, and we have Chex Mix together, just the two of us.

When I was four, my Grandpa spent a whole summer building me a playhouse with a big sandbox underneath. He made me a tire swing and pushes me lots of times in it. He pushes me real high, way up over his head. Now he spends all his extra time building new rooms on our house so that Mommy and I will have our own apartment.

I like living with my Grandpa and Grandma. We live out in the country with lots of room to play and fly kites. If we didn't live at Grandpa's house, we would have to live in a little apartment in town and I couldn't have my dog, my two house cats, my barn cats, and my gerbils. My Grandpa doesn't like cats very much, but he lets me keep two cats in the house and he buys lots of cat food and feeds the barn cats even when it's really cold out.

My Grandpa used to be a Boy Scout, and now he helps me with Cub Scouts. He helped me build my Pinewood Derby car and he's going to go camping with me this summer. He likes to tell me about things that happened when he was a little boy and when my mommy and uncle were little.

My Grandpa is really patient. When he is busy building things, he always takes time to start a nail so that I can pound it in. After he's spent all day mowing our big lawn he is really tired, but he will still hook my wagon up to the lawn mower and drive me all over the place.

My Grandpa loves Jesus, and he wants me to learn about Him too. Sometimes people on TV talk about kids from single parent families. I'm not one of them because I have three parents in my family. I hope that as I get older, Grandpa will teach me all the stuff he knows about wood and first-aid and everything else he knows about. My Grandpa isn't my Father, but I wouldn't trade him for all the dads in the world.

Dad, never underestimate the power you have—in your household and beyond. You have the potential to influence and shape generations.

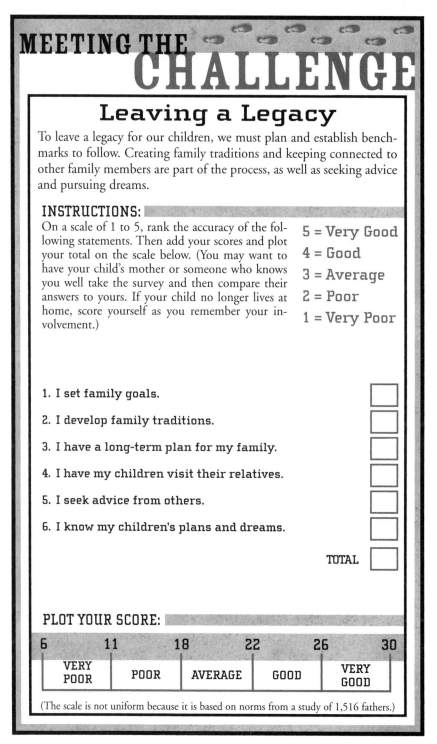

MEETING THE CHALLENGE

Leaving a Legacy

To leave a legacy for our children, we must plan and establish benchmarks to follow. Creating family traditions and keeping connected to other family members are part of the process, as well as seeking advice and pursuing dreams.

INSTRUCTIONS:

On a scale of 1 to 5, rank the accuracy of the following statements. Then add your scores and plot your total on the scale below. (You may want to have your child's mother or someone who knows you well take the survey and then compare their answers to yours. If your child no longer lives at home, score yourself as you remember your involvement.)

5 = Very Good

4 = Good

3 = Average

2 = Poor

1 = Very Poor

1. I set family goals. ☐

2. I develop family traditions. ☐

3. I have a long-term plan for my family. ☐

4. I have my children visit their relatives. ☐

5. I seek advice from others. ☐

6. I know my children's plans and dreams. ☐

TOTAL ☐

PLOT YOUR SCORE:

6	11	18	22	26	30
VERY POOR	POOR	AVERAGE	GOOD	VERY GOOD

(The scale is not uniform because it is based on norms from a study of 1,516 fathers.)

QUESTIONS FOR DISCUSSION AND REFLECTION

As you consider how you scored on this inventory, think about the following questions or discuss them with some other fathers.

1. What significant holiday or other family traditions do you remember from childhood? Have you continued any of them with your family?

2. What values and skills do you want to pass on to your children before they leave home?

3. How can you strengthen your relationship with your children in the coming year?

4. What legacy do you hope to leave for your children? What are you doing specifically to accomplish that?

5. Do you have a plan to help your children make a smooth transition into adulthood? If not, what should such a plan look like?

ACTION POINTS

Choose one of the following action points and commit to doing it before you go on to the next chapter (or your next group meeting).

1. Tell your children about the legacy you received from your father, your grandfather, or another father figure.

2. Ask your kids about their fondest, funniest, and their most sober or serious memories with you.

3. Intentionally do something this week that will make a lasting memory for your kids.

4. Be conscious of your impact on other children outside your family. Think of ways you can invest in their lives through a brief moment of attention, a word of praise, a kind gesture, or something more involved.

5. Start a habit of regularly writing to your children or grandchildren in a journal. Include your thoughts about life, important values, and the experiences that shaped you.

6. Sit down with your wife and talk about the top five values you want to transmit to your children and how you can build them into your life.

7. Craft—or revise—your personal mission statement and include items about your life as a father.

8. Prepare your children to handle the three most important decisions in life: (1) Where will I spend eternity? (2) Will I invest my time on things that have eternal value? (3) Whom will I marry?

9. Think about the challenges and new experiences each of your children will face in the coming year and how you can help prepare them. Then plan a time when you can talk with each child about those things and express your confidence in and love for him or her.

10. Devote five minutes each week to discussing an important virtue with your children (e.g., honesty, purity, generosity).

EACH ONE
MENTOR ONE

Truly, truly, I say to you, whoever believes in me
will also do the works that I do; and greater
works than these will he do, because I am going
to the Father.

JOHN 14:12

Several years ago, I was in our nation's capital to discuss a national initiative for fathers. The vice president invited me to meet with several other concerned leaders to discuss strategies that would encourage fathers to be more actively involved in the lives of their children. He wanted to know two things: How do we encourage and assist men to become more involved in the lives of their children? And who should take leadership in this effort?

I shared my perspective, and then I listened closely as the other leaders described what they believed our next steps should be. But as I reflected on who should lead this initiative to equip dads, a still, small voice spoke to me as clearly as any of the voices in the room. The Holy Spirit said, "Ken, they are describing *My church*. I have ordained the church to be the trainer and equipper of fathers."

I am convinced that our responsibility as dads of destiny expands beyond our own families. A faithful father has no choices about attending to the matters of the Father. One of those matters is clearly coming to the aid of the fatherless, the orphan, the widow, and the distressed. God is "a father to the fatherless, a defender of widows. . . . God sets the lonely in families" (Psalm 68:5–6 NIV). If we fail in our mission to build a bridge to the fatherless, then our churches, communities, cities, and nations as we know them will melt down.

A GLOBAL PERSPECTIVE

Kingsley Vander-Puije knows this well. He gives leadership to one of our partner organizations located in Ghana, Africa, called Father Care. Kingsley's father had eighteen children by sixteen different mothers. Kingsley didn't meet his father until he was twenty-three, a meeting that he describes as the most difficult, yet desired, of his life. During that meeting, his father flatly denied any knowledge of Kingsley or his mother. So Kingsley continued his search, and eventually learned that this man was, in fact, his father. In time his father apologized, and the two of them have established a relationship. Kingsley says, "I have become a source of comfort and a God-sent help. I believe that he wished our story could be rewritten!"

Kingsley believes father-child disconnectedness is the root cause of the chaotic violence that has plagued all of Africa. He believes that when children are rejected, abandoned, or abused by their fathers, they acquire a sense of worthlessness and animosity. Over time this animosity evolves into posturing and anger and then violence. Currently, the majority of African children do not know their fathers, and this is setting the stage for further conflict. As Kingsley says, "If we fail to address the brokenness between fathers and children, the future of Africa is bleak."

In America, we refer to children without fathers as fatherless. However, Kingsley calls them "the unfathered." It may seem like a simple difference in terminology, but the implications are profound. Calling a child fatherless puts the burden on the child, which is inappropriate as the child is in a situation he or she cannot control. However, if a child is unfathered, the child is not being attended to in a proper way, and the responsibility is placed on the father, as it should be.

A PERSONAL PERSPECTIVE

Some thirty years ago, I became friends with a young man in our church who needed intervention. Brian's parents had divorced, and his father was not involved in his life. Brian was figuring out his identity as a young man and a son. My wife, Dee, and I were newly married and had no children yet. We came to know Brian's family, and his mother was eager for me to spend some time with him.

Brian and I spent nearly every Saturday together, and I'll never forget the way he watched me and listened closely to everything I said. We never did anything extravagant—usually just shot baskets or hung out together. But that's when I realized that it's on God's heart to provide a male role model for the unfathered.

One day I sat down and wrote Brian a short note on a card. It wasn't anything profound or heartwarming. It said something like:

Dear Brian,

I'm looking forward to getting together again with you this Saturday. I've enjoyed our time together, and I just want you to know that you're a great guy to be around.

Your big brother,
Ken

I wrote nothing life-changing, but the next time I went to see Brian, I saw my hand-written note proudly displayed on his wall, along with posters of the sports heroes of the day. When I saw how proud he was of that note, I realized the impact I could have in Brian's life—and the lives of other unfathered men.

ANOTHER LEADER'S PERSPECTIVE

Glenn Jeffrey left a successful career in business to invest in the lives of America's fatherless through a church-based mentoring ministry called Life Coaches, which he founded. Its mission is to break the cycle of father absence by establishing mentors in the church. Glenn believes one of the missions of the local church is to become a place of refuge for the fatherless.

When Glenn first met Warren, the youth corrections facility described him as their "most incorrigible" kid. Warren's dad never lived at home, drank a lot, and rejected his son from the moment of his conception. At age eight, Warren started stealing cars. Later he ran with gangs, abused drugs, and showed little regard for anyone in authority. Two of Warren's older brothers were in prison, and Warren appeared to be headed the same way.

Glenn reached out to Warren for several years. During that time, Warren was in and out of corrections facilities; he left jobs that Glenn had helped him get and dropped out of barber school. For Glenn, Warren's setbacks were extremely discouraging. He viewed them as personal failures.

But eventually Warren yielded his life to Jesus and showed signs of change. He became an adult and moved on. Several years later he showed up at Glenn's door—clean-cut, happily married, a committed father, a successful businessman, and involved in leading a men's group at his church. Today Warren is reaching out and mentoring two fatherless young men in his church.

Glenn and I are convinced that if the church listens closely to cries of the fatherless, every fatherless child in America will soon have someone reaching out to them.

WHAT THE NUMBERS TELL US

Consider this: The Gallup organization regularly polls the faith practices of Americans. Their most recent poll found that 42 percent of the adult population say they have been "born again" or have trusted Jesus as their Savior.[1] According to our current census, there are 295,892,166 Americans. Of those, 97,352,124 are men between the ages of eighteen and seventy years of age. Stay with me. If we extract the number of born-again men (39 percent, as fewer men said they were born again when compared to women) from the total, we have 37,967,328 born-again men who can reach out to the fatherless. Our nation currently has over 25 million children under the age of eighteen who go to bed in a home without a father. What an impact we can make on these children, if each one mentors one.

With the fracture and brokenness in our communities and households, the time is ripe for those who have a relationship with the heavenly Father to reach out to the fatherless, one child at a time.

A KING'S HEART FOR FATHERLESS CHILDREN

I'm inspired by the story of a king who made the effort to reach out to a fatherless young man. The father in this case was King David. Saul and his son, Jonathan, had both been killed in battle. When David became king, he wanted to "show God's kindness" to "the house of Saul"

(2 Samuel 9:3 NIV). The only one left in Saul's family, however, was Jonathan's son, Mephibosheth, who was crippled.

David sent for Mephibosheth and said, "I will surely show you kindness for the sake of your father Jonathan. I will restore to you all the land that belonged to your grandfather Saul, and you will always eat at my table" (v. 7).

Mephibosheth had lost his father, his grandfather, and all of his inheritance. He even refers to himself as "a dead dog" who doesn't deserve the king's attention (v. 8). But David *honored* Mephibosheth by giving back his family's land and by recognizing him as one of his own sons. David gave this fatherless boy something much more valuable than any land or inheritance. He gave Mephibosheth his dignity. David effectively broke the curse of being unprotected and, in essence, fatherless.

Today other men are doing something similar. Consider the powerful impact we can have on a child, as seen in these two letters:

A twelfth grader writes:

My stepfather became my father when I was eight years old. My real father had died of cancer when I was six years old. My family was broken and needed healing. The Lord blessed us with my new father, Mark. He was like an angel sent from God. He, too, had lost his father when he was young, and he knew what my brothers and I were going through. He comforted us and gave us strength to continue.

When I was eleven, I was diagnosed with cancer. My family was devastated; just when we thought all of the turmoil was over, we realized it was only the beginning. The doctors decided I needed a bone marrow transplant. My stepfather, Mark, was a perfect match . . .

A father doesn't have to be someone who is biologically related to you. It is someone who would do anything for you and loves you with all of his heart and self. I pray that my father and I will remain this close throughout all of our lives and that we will only grow closer as time passes.

An eleventh-grade girl writes:

My biological father wasn't there for my first words, my first steps, my first anything. The person who was there was my uncle Craig. Uncle Craig was the one who taught me how to ride a bike, never losing patience when I didn't want to get on. He taught me how to drive, how to do everything a father should teach his child.

Uncle Craig has three children of his own and he's everything to them, and although he may have more important things to do, he makes time for me—no questions asked. My uncle Craig is a great man and a loving father. A father with three kids of his own with enough love for me, as well as them. He is the man who will meet my first date and the man who will walk me down the aisle at my wedding. He is my father and always will be. There is no one like him.

As sons of the Father, we must reach out to the fatherless within our sphere of influence and begin making a difference one life at a time. Each one mentor one. Let's begin today!

NOTES

Introduction: A Call to Action

1. The classic study that reviews the literature surrounding father absence is Sara McLanahan and Karen Booth, "Mother-Only Families: Problems, Prospects, and Politics," *Journal of Marriage and the Family* 51 (1989): 557–80. Additional studies that highlight the impact of father absence include Michael Lamb, *The Role of the Father in Child Development*, 3rd ed. (New York: Wiley, 1997); Sara McLanahan and Gary Sandefur, *Growing up with a Single Parent: What Hurts, What Helps* (Cambridge, Mass.: Harvard University Press, 1994); David Popenoe, *Life Without Father* (New York: The Free Press, 1996).

2. Kyle D. Pruett, *Fatherneed* (New York: The Free Press, 2000), 2.

3. Gallup Poll (1996), http://fathers.com/research/gallup/index.html.

4. Marie A. Bracki, Bonnie M. Dolson, and Kenneth Maurice, "Pre-Teen Gang Members: The Father Connection." Paper presented at the Annual Meeting of the American Psychological Association (105th, Chicago, Ill., August 15–19, 1997).

5. Frank A. Pedersen, Joan T. D. Suwalsky, Richard L. Cain, Martha J. Zaslow, and Beth A. Rabinovich, "Paternal Care of Infants During Maternal Separations: Associations with Father-Infant Interaction at One Year," *Psychiatry* 50 (August 1987): 203.

6. F. F. Furstenberg Jr. and K. M. Harris, "When and Why Fathers Matter: Impacts of Father Involvement on the Children of Adolescent Mothers," in *Young Unwed Fathers: Changing Roles and Emerging Policies,* ed. R. I. Lerman and T. H. Ooms (Philadelphia: Temple University Press, 1993).

7. John Snarey, *How Fathers Care for the Next Generation: A Four-Decade Study* (Cambridge, Mass.: Harvard University Press, 1993), 278.

8. Frederick Buechner, *Telling Secrets* (San Francisco: HarperCollins, 1991), 22.

Chapter 1: Dads of Destiny

1. C. S. Lewis, *The Abolition of Man* (New York: Macmillan, 1947), 101.

2. J. Jeremias, *The Prayers of Jesus* (Philadelphia: Fortress Press, 1964), 62.

3. Poem by Ken R. Canfield. Used by Permission. All rights reserved.

4. Gale H. Roid and Ken R. Canfield, "Measuring the Dimensions of Effective Fathering," *Educational and Psychological Measurement* 54 (Spring 1994): 212–17.

Chapter 2: Fill Their Emotional Cups

1. Jeffrey Marx, *Season of Life: A Football Star, a Boy, a Journey to Manhood* (New York: Simon & Schuster, 2003), 45.

2. Ibid., 100.

3. Jeffrey Marx, "He Turns Boys into Men," *Parade Magazine*, 29 August 2004, 7.

4. B. Rollins and D. Thomas, "Parental Support, Power, and Control Techniques in the Socialization of Children," in *Contemporary Theories about the Family,* ed. Wesley R. Burr, Rubin Hill, F. Ivan Nye, and I. L. Reiss, vol. 1. (New York: Free Press, 1986), 792.

5. Carla Cantor, "The Father Factor," *Working Mother*, June 1992, 41.

6. Christina Hoff Sommers, *The War Against Boys* (New York: Touchstone, 2000), 124–29.

7. Helen Colton, *The Gift of Touch* (New York: Seaview/Putnam, 1983), 102, quoted in Gary Smalley and John Trent, *The Blessing* (Nashville: Nelson, 1986), 40.

8. Gary Smalley and John Trent, *The Blessing* (New York: Pocket Books, a division of Simon & Schuster, 1990), 42.

9. Gordon MacDonald made these points in an address to a convocation of fatherhood leaders at Trinity University, Deerfield, Ill., June, 1992.

Chapter 4: Help Them Reach Out to Others

1. Rick Warren, *The Purpose-Driven Life* (Grand Rapids: Zondervan, 2002), 127.

2. Ibid., 287.

3. Ibid., 287.

4. Susan Bernadette-Shapiro, Diane Ehrensaft, and Jerrold Lee Shapiro, "Father Participation in Childcare and the Development of Empathy in Sons: An Empirical Study," *Family Therapy,* 23 (2): (1996), 77–93.

Chapter 5: Teach Discernment

1. Edith Schaeffer, *Ten Things Parents Must Teach Their Children—and Learn For Themselves* (Grand Rapids: Baker Books, 1994), 22.

2. Jim Fay, "Four Steps to Responsibility," cassette tape (Golden, Colo.: Love and Logic Press, Inc., 2207 Jackson St, Suite 102 80401-2300. Cline/Fay Institute, Inc., 1986).

3. Foster Cline and Jim Fay, *Parenting with Love and Logic* (Colorado Springs: Pinon Press, 1998).

4. David Blankenhorn, "Hardwired to Connect" (New York: Institute for American Values, 2003).

Chapter 6: Proactively Pass On Your Faith

1. Pauline Sawyers, "The Effects of Motivational Interviewing and Discussion on Father/Adolescent Religious Value Convergence" (PhD dissertation, University of New Mexico, 1998).

2. Walt Mueller, *Understanding Today's Youth Culture* (Wheaton, Ill.: Tyndale, 1994), 28–30.

3. Daniel Levinson, *The Seasons of a Man's Life* (New York: Ballantine, 1978), 59. For a more recent look beyond his book, see Daniel Levinson, "A Conception of Adult Development," *American Psychologist* (January 1986): 3–13.

4. Diana Mendley Rauner, *They Still Pick Me Up When I Fall: The Role of Caring in Youth Development and Community Life* (New York: Columbia University Press, 2000), 20–21.

5. William Gouge, *Of Domestical Duties* (London: STC:12119, 1622), 18.

6. Dr. Bill Beahm, a pastor and colleague of mine, came up with this four-step truth-teaching process that the National Center for Fathering uses in its Dads of Destiny training.

Chapter 7: Be Their Primary Educator

1. William Barclay, *Train Up a Child: Educational Ideals in the Ancient World*

(Philadelphia: Westminster, 1959), 236.

2. Richard Baxter, *Practical Works* (London, 1673: 4:231).

3. See http://www.fathers.com/articles/articles.asp?id=653&cat=49.

4. For more information on WatchDOGS, visit www.fathers.com/ watchdogs.

5. Edmund Morgan, *The Puritan Family: Religion and Domestic Relations in Seventeenth-Century New England* (New York: Harper & Row, 1966), 87.

6. Ibid., 88.

7. Ibid., 90.

Chapter 8: Walk Your Talk

1. Jesus spoke these words in a culture where apprentices were common. A son would be apprenticed to his father's trade. The son would watch his father at work and practice the skills that his father performed. Over time, a wise father revealed to his son all the secrets of the trade, and when the time was right, the son would take over the father's business. This tradition of vocational apprenticeships has been a standard for centuries, and though the industrial and technological revolutions have changed life dramatically, there are some elements of apprenticing we must apply to our fathering skills.

2. Gordon Dalbey, *Healing the Masculine Soul* (Dallas: Word, 1989), 174.

3. Ibid., 175.

Chapter 9: Foster Self-Control

1. Stephen R. Covey, *The 7 Habits of Highly Effective Families* (New York: Golden Books Publishing, 1997), 44.

2. Pruett, *Fatherneed*, 50.

3. Richard Swenson, MD, *The Overload Syndrome* (Colorado Springs: NavPress, 1998), 165.

Chapter 10: Build a Godly Legacy

1. Milton Siegel, letter to the author, c. 2000.

2. James Dobson made this statement during a Promise Keepers conference in June 1993, Boulder, Colo.

Conclusion: Each One Mentor One

1. See http://www.gallup.com.

ABOUT THE AUTHOR

Dr. Ken Canfield is a research scholar who founded the National Center for Fathering as a virtual training center to equip fathers, grandfathers, and father figures. His work has won national acclaim, and he has appeared on *The Oprah Winfrey Show, Focus on the Family,* NBC's *Today Show*, and ABC's *World News Tonight.* Canfield's fathering-related articles have appeared in numerous periodicals (both scientific and popular). He earned his BA from Friends University, an MCS from University of British Columbia-Regent College, and a PhD from Kansas State University. Ken and his wife, Dee, have been married twenty-nine years. They have five children and reside in Overland Park, Kansas.

fathers.com

The National Center for Fathering (NCF) was founded in 1990 by Dr. Ken Canfield in response to the dramatic trend towards fatherlessness in America. Providing research-based training and practical resources, the Center is the *only* national organization focused on equipping men to be the involved fathers, grandfathers, and father figures children need. The Center partners with and provides resources for state and local social service agencies, schools, faith communities, and everyday dads, reaching more than one million dads annually through our training efforts.

Dr. Canfield has written several highly respected books which are vital resources for fathers, including *The 7 Secrets of Effective Fathers* (Tyndale) and *The Heart of a Father* (Northfield). Ken's popular seminars incorporate teachings from these books and more into dynamic, practical and memorable instruction. The Center has also helped to launch two events where fathers and their teenage children can dedicate a day to strengthening their relationships—the *Father-Daughter Summit* and *Passage* (for boys).

Other efforts to equip dads include: Ken's free *fathers.com weekly* e-mail and daily *Today's Father* radio program, our small-group training and Train-the-Trainer workshops, and our award-winning Web site, www.fathers.com. The Center also provides leading edge fathering programs including the Urban Father-Child Partnership, the Father of the Year Essay Contest, WatchDOGS (Dads of Great Students), Coach DADS, R.E.A.D. to Kids and Fathering Court.

The National Center is funded through the sale of fathering resources and the generous support of foundations and thousands of individuals who believe that involved fathers are critical to strong families.

JOIN A SMALL GROUP

One powerful step in renewing fatherhood is simply to get dads talking about being dads. A step beyond that is organizing a small group that meets occasionally or regularly. The questions in this book were designed precisely for that purpose.

We also recommend our DADS OF DESTINY small-group program, which is simply the best systematic approach to transforming families by transforming fathers. The program now has three 6-week studies—Foundations in Fathering, Going the Distance, and Communicating with Your Family. Each study includes required reading on fatherhood topics, regular homework, interaction and activities with family members, Bible study and written responses to questions, as well as the regular meetings with other men who hold you accountable for what you have learned.

Stay in touch with us at the National Center for continuing assistance in your fathering journey. You can sign up to receive Ken's free e-mail, *fathers.com weekly*, at www.fathers.com

National Center for Fathering
P.O. Box 413888
Kansas City, Missouri 64141
Phone: (800) 593-3237
Fax: (913) 384-4665
e-mail: dads@fathers.com
Web site: http://www.fathers.com